The
New Guide
to
Mushrooms

THE
NEW GUIDE
TO
MUSHROOMS

THE ULTIMATE GUIDE TO IDENTIFYING,
PICKING AND USING MUSHROOMS

PETER JORDAN

LORENZ BOOKS

Disclaimer
The publishers and authors cannot accept responsibility
for any identification of any mushroom made by users
of this guide. Although many species are edible for
many people, some species cause allergic reactions or
illness to some people: these are totally unpredictable.
Therefore, the publishers and authors cannot take
responsibility for any effects from eating
any wild mushroom.

Paperback edition first published in 1998 by Lorenz Books
27 West 20th Street, New York, NY 10011

LORENZ BOOKS are available for bulk purchase for sales promotion
and for premium use. For details, write or call the sales director,
Lorenz Books, 27 West 20th Street, New York, NY 10011;
(800) 354-9657

© Anness Publishing Limited 1995, 1996

Lorenz Books is an imprint of
Anness Publishing Inc.

ISBN 1-85967-735-5

Publisher: Joanna Lorenz
Project Editor: Clare Nicholson
Designer: Michael Morey
Illustrator: Adam Abel
Indexer: Alex Corrin

Printed and bound in Singapore by
Star Standard Industries Pte. Ltd.

1 3 5 7 9 10 8 6 4 2

CONTENTS

INTRODUCTION   **6**

Foreword   8

What are mushrooms?   10

The different parts of mushrooms   12

Where to collect mushrooms   14

When to collect mushrooms   16

How to collect mushrooms   18

Storing mushrooms   20

EDIBLE MUSHROOMS   **22**

POISONOUS MUSHROOMS   **96**

GLOSSARY   122

INDEX   124

BIBLIOGRAPHY   127

ACKNOWLEDGEMENTS   128

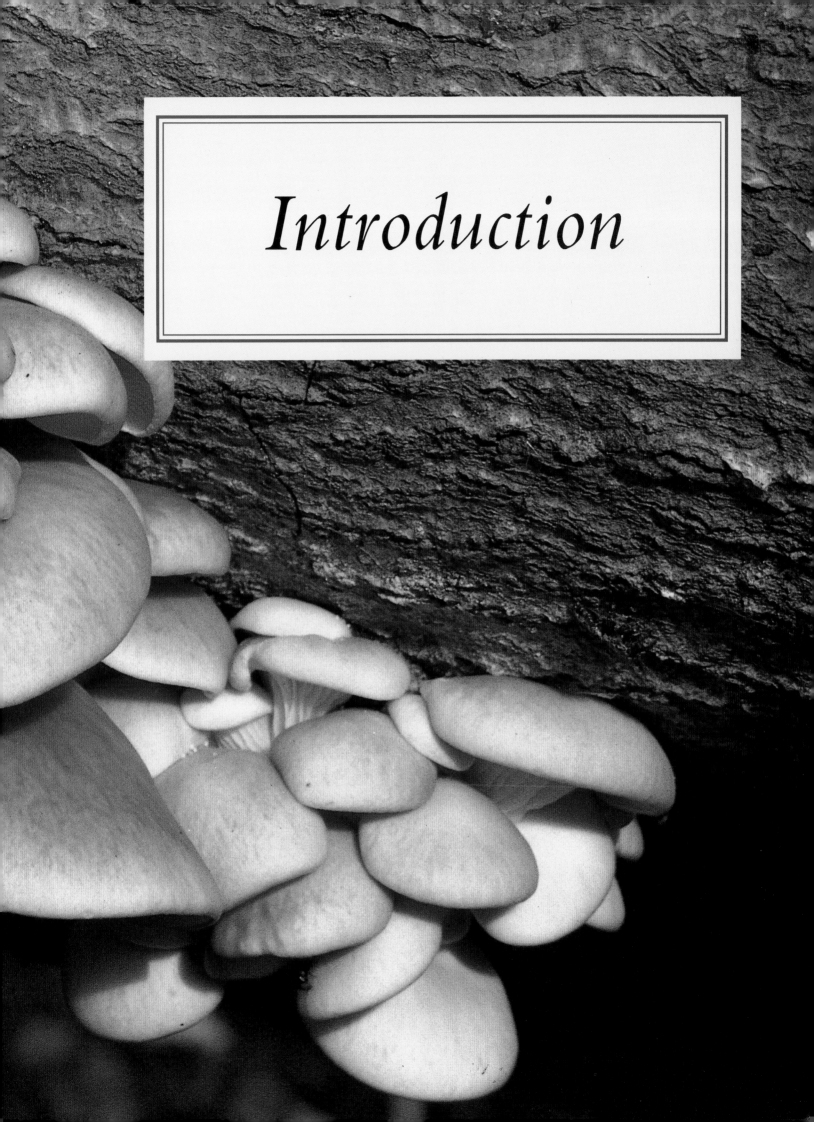

Introduction

FOREWORD

I was introduced to wild mushrooms by my grandfather who was a farmer in Norfolk, England. From the age of four I would go out in the fields with him to collect not only what he described as field mushrooms, but also some weird and wonderful looking mushrooms which I thought were poisonous – they certainly looked menacing to a child. However, he taught me one very good lesson: as long as you can identify absolutely accurately what you are picking you will be safe. From these early beginnings developed a lifetime's interest in mushrooms.

The excitement of walking along a woodland path in the autumn, and finding in front of you two or three perfectly formed ceps is wonderful. During fifty years as a mushroom hunter, I have graduated from the relatively common horse and field mushrooms to the more exotic chanterelles and ceps. I am still excited when I find the first morels of the spring, or the year's first patch of chanterelles hidden in the leaf mold; of course, the more elusive the mushroom, like the horn of plenty or the winter chanterelle, the greater the excitement. Imagine the ultimate triumph of finding your first giant puffball – it's head actually bigger than your own! But, as well as providing excitement and good eating, mushrooms can be dangerous; correct identification is the key to successful mushroom collecting.

The fruits, nuts and mushrooms of autumn are obvious and most are easy to spot. But have you ever realized that the winter, spring and summer can be as productive – at least as far as mushrooms are concerned? Mushrooms are one of the few wild treasures available nearly all the year round. Even on a crisp winter's day you can find a bouquet of silver-gray oyster mushrooms or the wonderful velvet shank growing out of a tree stump and it is so much more satisfying to pick them like this than from a supermarket shelf. Because, of course, the excitement of finding the mushrooms is closely followed by the satisfaction of cooking them within hours if not minutes of their harvest.

Identifying mushrooms, utterly essential though it is, can be frustrating if you have to wade through hundreds of illustrations, many of which look the same. This book is designed to make that task easier. It illustrates the best of the edible mushrooms, and so will help you pick your way wisely through the year's mushrooms, alerting you not only to a season's treasures, but also to the poisonous lookalikes and really deadly fungi that all too often grow alongside innocent and delicious mushrooms. The section that deals with the poisonous species will help identification and give the faint-hearted confidence to take their finds back to the kitchen. But do follow the advice given in this guide carefully. If clear identification is not possible from this book, consult others – the bibliography lists some of the best. And remember that the best advice of all is: if in doubt do not collect a mushroom and never, ever, eat anything you cannot identify with certainty.

Peter Jordan

WHAT ARE MUSHROOMS?

The terms mushrooms, toadstools and fungi (singular fungus) are often used loosely and interchangeably. However, this can be misleading.

The fungi are a very large group of organisms and include molds, yeasts, mushrooms and "toadstools". None of these organisms contain the green pigment chlorophyll, so they cannot make their own food by the process known as photosynthesis.

Mushrooms are usually defined as the edible, spore-producing bodies of some fungi. In contrast, the term toadstool was applied to the spore-producing bodies of those fungi that are not only inedible but may also be highly dangerous. It has ceased to be used, in part because the basis for definition were often dangerously inaccurate. So, while the terms fungus and fungi have a very precise scientific meaning, mushroom and toadstool do not. In this book mushroom is used whether, or not, the fruit body of that particular fungus is edible. It is used to cover a large number of different types of fungi such as mushrooms, boletes, bracket fungi, puff balls and cap fungi.

Ascomycetes

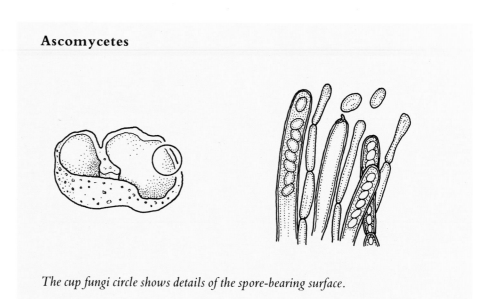

The cup fungi circle shows details of the spore-bearing surface.

Basidiomycetes

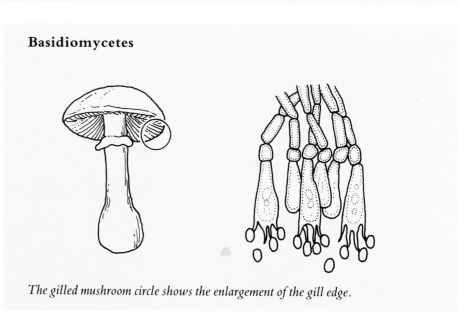

The gilled mushroom circle shows the enlargement of the gill edge.

Tuber aestivum, *the summer truffle, an example of an ascomycete fungus.*

The fungi in this book divide into two main groups: the Ascomycetes and the Basidiomycetes. The Ascomycetes produce spores that are spread by the wind. Among this group are many of the cup fungi, including the common morel and *Gyromitra esculenta*. Because the wind spreads the spore of many of these mushrooms, it is worth remembering when you find some morels, for example, to check downwind and you will almost certainly find some more.

The second group, and by far the largest as far as the collector is concerned, is the Basidiomycetes, which includes the large and well-known Agaric and Bolete families. These two families, in fact, form sub-divisions within the group.

A mushroom of the Agaric type is illustrated here with the various parts clearly identified. This is a gilled mushroom and sometimes grows from an egg-shaped volval cup. Care must be taken when dealing with any mushroom that grows from a volval cup, because this is how the *Amanitas*, the most deadly of all mushroom species, grow.

Parts of the Agaric-type fungi

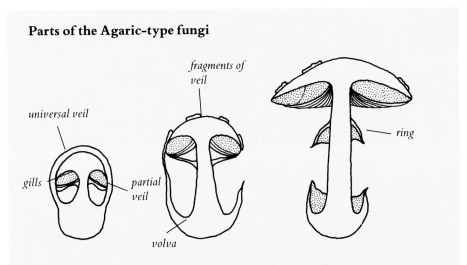

The universal veil encloses the whole mushroom and the partial veil covers the gills. As the mushroom grows the universal veil ruptures to leave a volva and fragments on the cap, and the partial veil ruptures to leave a ring on the stem.

Parts of the Boletus-type fungi

A second sub-division is the Boletes. Instead of having gills, mushrooms in this group have tubes and pores which vary widely in color. Boletes, like Agarics, are fleshy and decay readily. This separates them from the Polypores. It is important to note their color because this can be a clear indicator of the mushrooms you have found. The cep is the best-known member of this group.

A third group of fungi illustrated in this book is Aphyllophorales. This group includes the polypores and chanterelles and a number of other mushrooms that have irregular shapes. A number of fungi fall into this group, for example, the hedge-hog fungus, which, instead of gills, has tiny spines from which it gets its name. Another member of the group is the cauliflower fungus. It may look odd, but it is a wonderful find from a culinary point of view. Other unusual types are the beefsteak fungus and the sulphur polypore or chicken of the woods. Both are excellent for cooking as well as being quite spectacular when you encounter them in the wild.

Examples of the two types of fungi which form sub-divisions of the Basidiomycetes. The horse mushroom (above) and the cep (right).

Cauliflower fungus is an example of the third major group of fungi, the Aphyllophorates.

THE DIFFERENT PARTS OF MUSHROOMS

When you start collecting wild mushrooms it is important to consider carefully what it is that you are collecting. The mushroom itself can be divided into various parts. From both the collecting and culinary points of view the cap of the fruit body is the most important part. The shape, size and color of the cap can show tremendous variation within a species, which is one of the reasons why mushrooms are so difficult to identify accurately. It is also important to note whether the cap has gills or pores, what the colors of these are and whether they are crowded or open.

Stems can also vary considerably and they, too, can often be an important indicator of precisely which mushroom you have discovered. Does the stem have a veil or not? The

base of the stem is a vital means of identification, particularly if you have any doubts about the specimens you have found. If you are not sure what it is, carefully dig out the mushroom so that you can see the base of the stem. If there is any sign of a volval cup have nothing more to do with the mushroom. Incidentally, whatever the mushroom that you are digging up proves to be, be careful not to do too much damage to the mycelial threads that connect it to the rest of the underground part of the fungus.

The color of the mushroom's flesh is another important means of identification. Not only should you look at the whole mushroom, you should also cut it through in cross-section. Some important details, such as whether the stem is hollow, can of

course, only be seen in cross-section. In some species the stems change color quite dramatically when they are cut. Take note of any such changes, because they can be a reliable identification feature in certain types of mushroom.

Spore prints are also a good means of identifying mushrooms and are very easy to do. Take a cap of a mature specimen of a mushroom and place it on black and white paper on top of a container. Cover with a glass or shallow bowl. Then let sit for a few hours to a day so the mushroom sheds all its spores and you will have a very clear spore print. If you do not know what color the spore will be, put down a piece of black paper and overlay part of it with white paper. Then place the cap so that it is half on the black paper and half on the white.

Examples of different shapes of stems

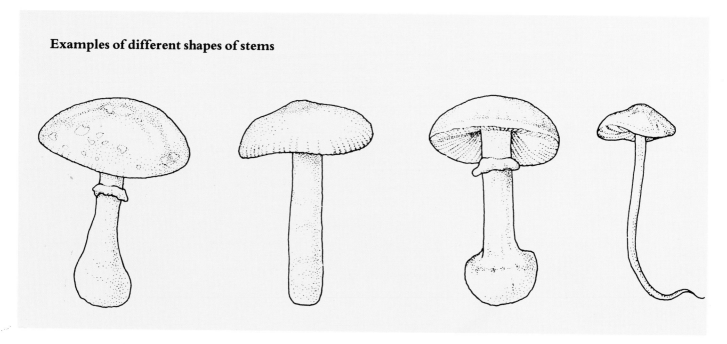

LEFT *To take a spore print you will need a mature specimen, white, or black and white paper and a container to place it on.*

LEFT BELOW *Leave the mushroom in a warm place for a few hours to one day.*

LEFT BOTTOM *Do not use just black paper because it will not show up if the spore print is a dark color.*

BELOW *Taking a spore print is a very reliable way of making an accurate identification.*

WHERE TO COLLECT MUSHROOMS

Always take care when you are out mushroom collecting that you do not trespass. Always get permission from the landowner before you go on to any land that is not open to the public. When you are mushroom collecting be careful of the surrounding countryside and its animals, otherwise not only will you soon get a bad reputation, but you will give other collectors a similar reputation whether they deserve it or not.

Most people limit their mushroom hunting to meadows, but these have suffered from being overenriched with nitrates, which have denuded many previously good mushroom-hunting territories. If you want to find meadowland mushrooms it is best to examine those meadows and marshes that have been treated with natural organic fertilizers and not nitrates. But why restrict yourself to meadowland species when eighty per cent of fungi grow in association

with trees? Woods and forests are the places where you should really be looking for mushrooms, but only, of course, once you have made sure that you will not be trespassing.

Established woods and forests containing a wide variety of species provide the very best places for mushroom collecting and it is in such areas that the vast majority of species are to be found. Many of these fungi have a symbiotic relationship with trees and their roots, with some fungi growing only with a particular species of tree, while other fungi can be found in association with a number of different trees. For example, many boletes grow only with one type of tree such as the species of *Suillus* which only grow with conifers, or the species of *Leccinum* which are very specific: *Leccinum versipelle* grows with birch and *L. aurantiacum* with aspen. Chanterelles on the other hand can grow effectively with birch,

pine, oaks or even beech trees.

Soil type is also important. Although many trees grow on a variety of soils, you will find that some fungi will only grow with a particular tree on a particular soil, rather than across the whole range of soils on which the tree grows. For example the bay boletes grows under beech trees or under conifers on acid soils, and the panther cap grows under beech trees on alkaline soils.

ABOVE *The early morning is prime mushroom hunting time.*

OPPOSITE *Do not restrict your mushroom hunting to meadows and woodlands: marshes and heathland can be surprisingly productive too.*

LEFT *Many mushrooms grow in rings, some of which reach several yards wide.*

WHEN TO COLLECT MUSHROOMS

Most people associate mushrooms with the autumn, but, in fact, they grow throughout the year.

The spring brings morels and the St George's mushroom *Calocybe gambosa*. The fairy ring mushroom, *Marasmius oreades*, also appears quite early in the year. The first of the summer mushrooms is usually the field mushroom, *Agaricus campestris*. Another mushroom to appear fairly early in summer is the chicken of the woods, *Laetiporus sulphureus*, indeed it often catches collectors unawares with its early appearance. When, or indeed if, there is a spell of hot weather, there is usually little to be found, but these conditions are, nevertheless, important, because they help the mushrooms' underground mycelial threads to mature before the autumn's great burst of growth. If the weather is mild, the autumn can extend into early winter. The first touches of frost may herald the com-

ing of winter, but they can often bring exciting finds of both the brick cap, *Na, Naematoloma sublateritium*, and the blewit, *Lepista nuda*. Both these species will continue until the weather turns quite frosty.

When winter takes hold, most

people give up and just look forward to the next mushroom season. But don't be fooled: on mild winter days in more temperate zones, go out searching and you will be surprised at what you find. Oyster mushrooms, *Pleurotus ostreatus*, will continue to grow almost right through the winter, together with the tree ear, *Auricularia auricula*, and the velvet shank, *Flammulina velutipes*. Finding these can make a cold winter walk tremendously exciting, and shows that even in the depth of winter you can enjoy a dish with ingredients freshly picked from fields and woods.

The mushroom collector's year never ends and even when you're not actually hunting, always be on the lookout for new spots. Use winter walks to examine pastures and woodlands that you have not been to before, to see if they give any clues as to what they are likely to produce when spring comes again.

It may seem surprising, but time of day is most important to the mushroom collector. This is because mushrooms grow almost exclusively

during the hours of darkness. As a result, the best specimens are picked when they are fresh in the early morning before the rising temperature of the day has brought out the flies to lay their eggs, so giving rise to insect infestation, or the animals of the woods and fields have had their pickings of the overnight growth, which can be quite amazing in its quantity.

It is also worth revisiting a place you have picked after two or three days, because the mushrooms will usually have grown back. Ceps are known to grow back to a weight of 1¾ lb within two or three days of the first growth having been picked – an enormous rate of growth by any standard.

It is useful to keep a diary of what you find, when and where you found it, and what the climatic conditions were, as this will give you a key to subsequent seasons and help you develop a knowledge and understanding of your local area. Noting climatic conditions is also interesting as well as useful. Good fungal growth needs periods of damp, but also periods of dry and cold, as the mycelial threads seem to benefit from a degree of stratification which, in turn, gives rise to better fruiting, and thus to better collecting.

OPPOSITE ABOVE *Chicken of the woods grows from late spring to early autumn.*

OPPOSITE BELOW *Oyster mushrooms continue to grow through the winter.*

ABOVE *The poisonous* Clitocybe rivulosa *appears in summer and autumn.*

LEFT *Blewits.*

HOW TO COLLECT MUSHROOMS

Very little equipment is needed for mushroom collecting. Tough outdoor clothes and a strong pair of boots are essential and you should make sure that your jacket or parka has a pocket large enough to carry a small field guide. It is not an exaggeration: some mushrooms are just too dangerous to take home. You may find a wide-brimmed hat useful to wear in the autumn, as the days shorten and the sun is low. It is easier to spot those interesting little humps and bumps that could well prove to be an exciting find if you are not having to shade your eyes with your hand all the time.

One or two baskets are, of course, essential. They should be light, easy to carry and not too open in weave.

A sharp knife and brush are also important, the knife to cut the mushroom's stem through cleanly and the brush to remove obvious dirt and debris such as pine needles and leaf mold. Cleaning your specimens as you pick them will mean there is less to do when you get home. Several plastic bags or disposable gloves are also essential items to take with

OPPOSITE
Results of a successful morning's mushroom collecting.

RIGHT *A selection of handmade baskets.*

you. You can put these over your hands when handling any specimens about which you are doubtful. Don't forget to throw them away after you have used them. A package of tissues or a cloth will also be useful as your hands can get quite dirty. You will also need them to clean your knife, as you should clean it each time you use it.

The final item of equipment is a good strong stick. You can use it to part ferns and undergrowth to see if any mushrooms are hidden there. It will be handy to turn over any specimens you may not wish to touch, as well as being useful as a tool to dig out specimens so that you can check if they have volval cups or not.

When you find a specimen that you can identify with certainty and want to collect, it is best to cut

BELOW *A good knife is an essential part of any mushroom collector's equipment. Two of the knives here double as a brush as well.*

through its stem rather than dig it up. While it is possible to use the stems of mushrooms such as ceps and chanterelles, there is a danger of disturbing the mycelial threads if the entire mushroom is removed from the ground. The only possible exception to this rule is if you are confronted by what you think may be a poisonous mushroom. Then dig it up with your stick, being careful not to damage it. If there is anything that looks even remotely like a volval cup at the base of the stem, leave the whole specimen well alone.

Having cut through the mushroom's stem, wipe or brush clean the mushroom before putting it in your basket. As the basket starts to fill up, a layer of fern fronds will prevent the bottom mushrooms from becoming damaged.

STORING MUSHROOMS

There are certain times of the year when mushrooms grow in great profusion. It is important, therefore, to find ways to preserve this abundance for those times when few mushrooms grow. Preserving food is as old as time itself and long before refrigerators, salting and drying were used as methods of preservation. There are many different ways to store mushrooms and some species are more suited to a certain type of preservation than others. Informa-

laying them on cheesecloth trays in the sun can be quite sufficient. In cooler, less sunny regions, mushrooms can be dried on open trays in a warm stove, and on window sills. It is important to remember that the mushrooms must be dried thoroughly, which may take quite a few days and while drying is in progress an intense mushroomy smell will pervade wherever you are drying them.

In recent years, fruit dryers and

in strings in the kitchen. It is important to remember, however, that mushrooms such as morels could well have creepy-crawlies hiding inside so partially dry them somewhere before hanging them in your kitchen. This will prevent any wildlife dropping into your food. When the mushrooms are dry, carefully lay them on a sheet and pick the individual specimens over before placing them in airtight containers for storage. Don't waste any powder that

tion on the most suitable method for each species is given in the relevant individual entry.

Whatever method of storage you are going to use, it is important to select the very best of the mushrooms you have collected. Do be careful to make sure that they are completely free of insects because there is nothing worse when reconstituting dried mushrooms to find you have insects floating on the top of the water in which they are being reconstituted. Also make sure there are no twigs, leaves or other debris among them.

Drying preserves the flavor and color quite well, although unfortunately it often destroys the shape of the mushroom. There are several methods of drying. In warmer climates, slicing the mushrooms and

drying machines have become available. Some can take up to ten trays and are capable of drying a large quantity of wild mushrooms very effectively over several hours. The advantage of this is that it prevents the whole house smelling of mushrooms for days afterwards, and you can also be totally confident that your dried mushrooms are completely free of moisture. With this accelerated form of drying it is possible to dry even shaggy ink caps, so long as you use very young specimens. Ordinary drying methods are much too slow and they would collapse into an inky mess and probably ruin any other mushrooms you were drying with them.

Another effective way of drying mushrooms is to thread them with a needle and cotton and hang them up

may remain on the sheet, it can be stored separately and used to flavor soups and stews.

Dried mushrooms can be put directly into soups and stews, but for other dishes it is best to reconstitute them in lukewarm water for around twenty minutes. Do not use boiling water as this will impair the final flavor. The water in which they have been reconstituted can be used as stock or to make gravy, but, before you do so, pour it through a strainer to remove any extraneous matter or grit that might have been contained within the mushrooms.

An alternative to drying is freezing. Perhaps surprisingly, this is not a very good method of preserving mushrooms. For best results, make up the mushroom dishes and then freeze the finished dish or make up

RIGHT *Mushrooms that have been dried and preserved for later use.*

OPPOSITE FAR LEFT AND MIDDLE *It is essential to brush and wipe clean mushrooms before they are dried or stored.*

OPPOSITE NEAR RIGHT *A mushroom drier.*

mushroom butter. To do this, slice your mushrooms, add them to melted butter and freeze the result. Preserved like this you have the mushrooms and the butter for use with sauces, to flavor various dishes and to add to your meat or fish dishes as a topping.

Salting is one of the oldest methods of preserving food. It works extremely well for mushrooms. The most important thing to remember is to have clean, fresh mushrooms. The quantities required are one part salt to three parts mushrooms. It is important to layer the mushrooms and salt alternately, and make sure the final layer of mushrooms is completely covered with salt. Use containers that the salt will not corrode. Although a sterilized jar is best, you could also use plastic containers.

When preserving mushrooms in this way you will eventually have a lot of seasoned juice and you will not need to use salt in any dish you make using salted mushrooms.

Mushrooms can be pickled in either oil or good vinegar. It is most important when using this method to clean the mushrooms well and then blanch them. If you are pickling them with vinegar, remember that the better the vinegar, the better the results will be, so it is not worth putting good mushrooms in inferior vinegar. The same applies if you are pickling mushrooms in oil. It is also a good idea to put peppercorns and half a dozen cloves of garlic into each jar, together with two or three bay leaves. Make sure the containers you use have a good seal, and when they are filled, seal tightly.

Once the seals have been broken, use the contents fairly quickly. And it is a good idea to keep the container in the fridge while you are doing so. Even when you have finished the mushrooms, the oil or vinegar in which they have been stored will make a wonderful dressing. If you preserve mushrooms by pickling, you must remember to sterilize everything you use. You can do this by immersing all your utensils in boiling water, or by using a sterilizing solution. Boiling water is probably best as there is always a danger that the sterilizing solution might affect the taste of the mushrooms. Remember, too, to keep a watchful eye on your pickled mushrooms for any sign of moldiness. If there is, discard the top few mushrooms and use the rest fairly quickly.

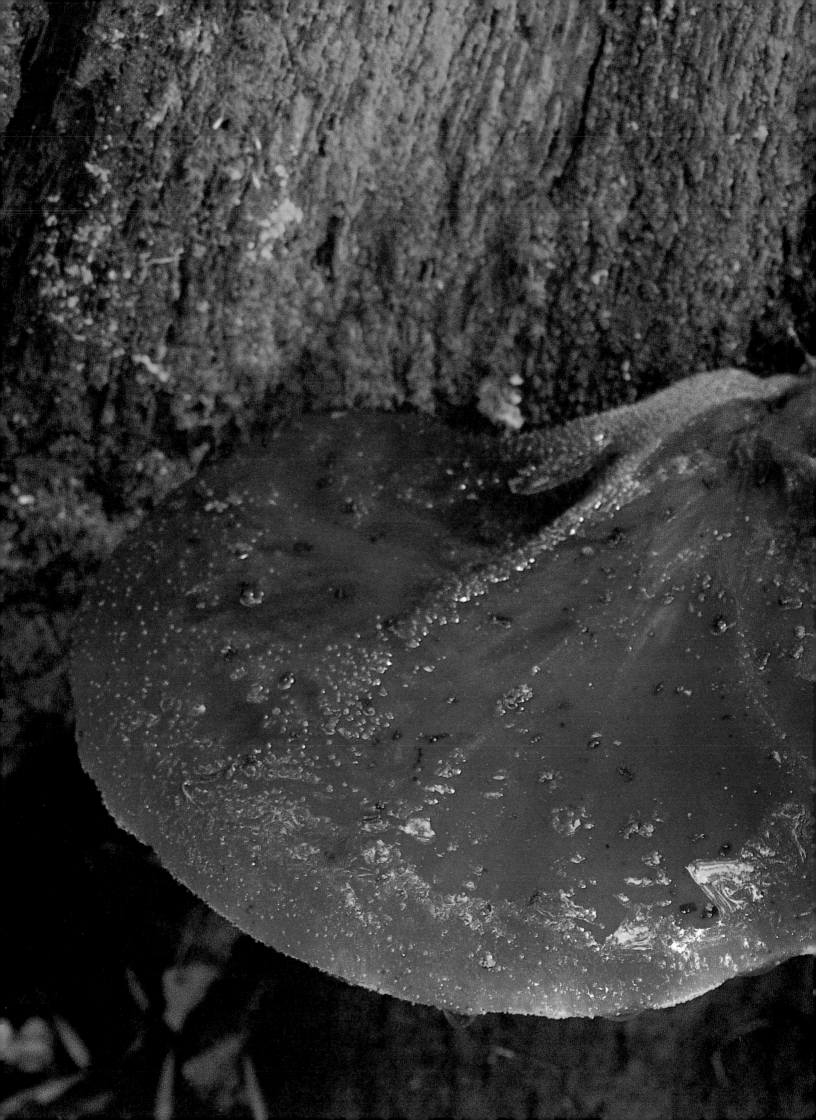

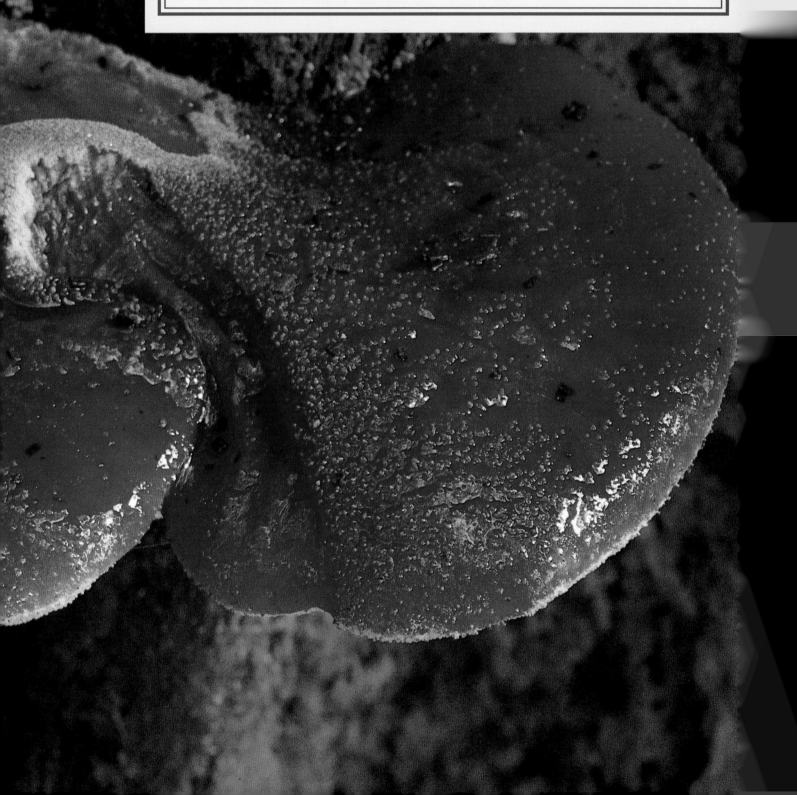

Edible Mushrooms

INTRODUCTION

This section illustrates and describes the best of the edible mushrooms that grow in our fields and woods. There are in fact over a thousand edible species and but only a small proportion of these are prized for their flavor and texture, and although personal taste will vary many consider the finest to include the cep *Boletus edulis*, bay bolete *Boletus badius*, morels *Morchella elata* and *esculenta*, chanterelle *Cantherellus cibarius* and chicken of the woods *Laetiporus sulphureus*. To enable identification each entry has a description of the mushroom in question, information on its habitat and season of growth, as well as hints on storage and cooking preparation for when you return home with a full basket.

As you learn about mushrooms you will become more respectful of the rules of identification. No mushroom looks exactly like another, and sometimes the differences are great within the same species. Many species have poisonous lookalikes, which are also mentioned here. Take particular care with such mushrooms. It is also essential that you never pick immature specimens for identification, because only with mature specimens can you be sure of an accurate identification.

Mushrooms are quite rich and even edible ones can cause stomach upsets. Some people seem more prone to these than others, so be careful if you are serving a mushroom dish to guests.

Although cultivated mushrooms can be eaten raw, all others should be cooked first. Mushrooms such as honey fungus *Armillaria mellea*, wood blewit *Lepista nuda*, field blewit *Lepista saeva*, and the morels *Morchella elata* and *esculenta* all contain a small amount of poison which is removed by cooking.

One of the best ways to learn about mushrooms is to go on a foray led by an expert. Not only will you have the chance to question the expert about the location, type and size of the various mushrooms that you find, but, at the end of the foray, you will have a chance to examine what everybody else has found and have them identified by the expert. In this way you will have an opportunity to see far more species than you would if you had just gone out collecting on your own. Forays are run by many organizations, including mycological societies, local nature trusts and local experts who organize them on an ad-hoc basis. Details of forays can usually be found through these groups and they may also be advertised in the local paper.

Enjoy your mushroom collecting, but don't take any risks with mushrooms you cannot identify.

PREVIOUS PAGE *Beefsteak fungus,* Fistulina hepatica. *Although these mushrooms are usually found at the base of tree trunks they can grow high up on the branches.*

LEFT *Field blewit,* Lepista saeva.

OPPOSITE *Amethyst deceiver,* Laccaria amethystea, *is a tasty mushroom that has a long season from late summer to early winter.*

Agaricus arvensis

HORSE MUSHROOM

This is one of the larger varieties of mushroom. It is quite meaty in texture and has a very distinctive anise smell. Horse mushrooms are best picked when they are young because not only are they soon attacked by insects, but also the flesh becomes dark brown with age and will turn any cooked dish muddy brown in color.

*mature gills
turn dark brown*

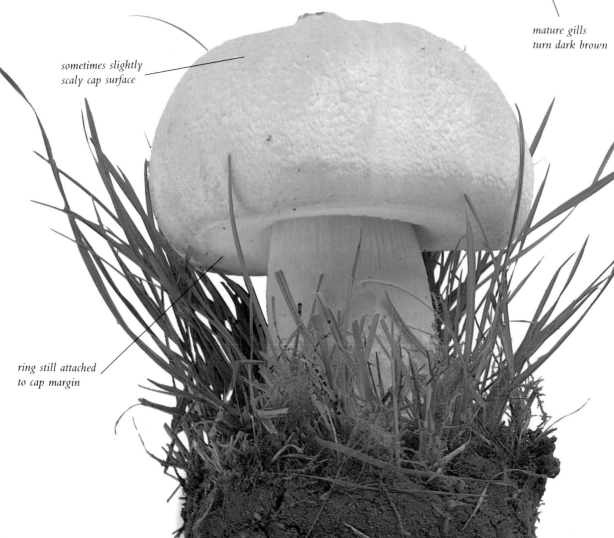

*sometimes slightly
scaly cap surface*

*ring still attached
to cap margin*

These mushrooms tend to come up in the same fields year after year, so having once found a good growth of horse mushrooms keep watching in future years.

The horse mushroom often has yellowish markings on the cap. When you find one like this, check it particularly carefully to ensure that it is not, in fact, the yellow stainer, *Agaricus xanthodermus*, which will make you very ill if you eat it. This mushroom is dealt with in detail in the section on poisonous mushrooms so you can compare the two. Unlike the yellow stainer, the horse mushroom does not color when pressed or cut; the yellow coloring of the cap is its natural color.

IDENTIFICATION
The cap can be from 4–9¾ in across. It is domed at first, but eventually expands to a fully convex shape. It is white but yellows with age. The stem is 3–4 in and has a large double ring. It may become hollow with age. The gills, which are white at first, turn a delicate pink and eventually dark brown in mature specimens. The flesh is thick and white but darkens with age and can become a little woolly lower down the stem. It has a distinct smell of anise. The spore print is dark brown.

HABITAT AND SEASON
Horse mushrooms favor grassland and pasture, particularly, as the name suggests, that where cattle or horses have grazed. Grassy roadsides are often good places to look. The season is from midsummer to quite late autumn and they often grow in quite large rings.

STORAGE
These mushrooms dry well, but it is important to check thoroughly that they are insect free. Slice and then dry either with open driers or with an electric drier.

PREPARATION AND COOKING HINTS
These mushrooms make wonderful meals, provided, of course, that they are not infested with insects. Remember, too, if you are using older specimens when the flesh has turned dark brown, that they will change the color of your dish.

ABOVE *The yellow stainer.*

ABOVE LEFT *The horse mushroom prefers open meadows or woodland edges.*

BELOW *This specimen has a fully expanded cap when mature.*

Agaricus augustus
THE PRINCE

The prince is a good mushroom to find: not only does it look attractive, but it also has a lovely flavor and tastes delicious. These mushrooms grow in deciduous and coniferous woodland, and in dense groups rather than rings, in western North America.

IDENTIFICATION
The cap is 4–9¾ in across. Button-shaped at first, it opens to a convex form and is often irregular in shape. It is light brown in color and has clearly marked rings of brown fibrous scales joining in the center. The stem is 4–7¾ in, off-white with small scales and a large floppy ring. The gills are off-white at first, turning dark brown with age. The flesh is thick, white and smells mushroomy. The spore print is brown.

HABITAT AND SEASON
The prince grows mainly in coniferous and deciduous woods, often in clumps. The season is late summer to late autumn.

STORAGE
As these mushrooms grow fairly large, make sure you have good specimens before slicing and drying them in the usual way. This is a good mushroom to store for winter use as it has an intensity of flavor which will enhance any mushroom dish.

PREPARATION AND COOKING HINTS
A nice mushroom that needs very little preparation. The stem tends to be quite fibrous, so is best discarded. The cap does not need peeling, just wipe lightly with a damp cloth before slicing. The prince makes an extremely good addition to omelets, but is also nice on its own.

cap surface always with flattened scales

ABOVE *The prince is usually found at the edges of woods, clearings or pathsides, rarely very far from trees.*

large floppy ring

stem usually strongly scaly

Agaricus bisporus

Agaricus bisporus smells and tastes very similar to the field mushroom. It is believed to be the species from which most of the cultivated varieties come. It can grow in quite large quantities and is mostly found on wasteground and compost heaps. It is quite common.

IDENTIFICATION

The cap is 2–4 in across, button-shaped before opening almost flat. It is whitish to mid-brown in color with flaky scales. The stem is 1¼–2 in and white, with a distinct ring below the cap. It has pink gills which become darker with age. The flesh is white, bruising slightly reddish and it has a distinct mushroomy smell. The spore print is brown.

ABOVE AND BELOW Agaricus bisporus *is the species that cultivated varieties come from. The button, cup and flat mushrooms, that are widely available, are the different stages of growth of this mushroom.*

HABITAT AND SEASON

It grows on compost heaps, in garden waste and beside roads, occasionally on the edges of hedges and small plantations, but very rarely in grass. The season is quite early in the spring through to late autumn.

STORAGE

This mushroom tends to be quite small and dries well, either whole or cut. It is full of flavor.

PREPARATION AND COOKING HINTS

Because this mushroom often grows on compost heaps or in rough ground, it is best to wipe the cap very thoroughly, cutting off the bottom of the stem and slicing through.

Agaricus campestris

FIELD MUSHROOM

The field mushroom is probably the best known of all wild mushrooms. Years ago fields were often carpeted with these small white mushrooms, but due to changes in farming technology and the greater use of herbicides, pesticides and, particularly, nitrates, many of the wonderful pastures where field mushrooms grew have disappeared. If you are lucky enough to have some old meadows and pasture near you, keep an eye open for a wonderful feast that can come at any time from quite early in the summer through to autumn. These mushrooms are best picked early in the morning, not only to beat other mushroom collectors, but also to ensure that they have not yet been attacked by insects.

IDENTIFICATION

The cap is 1¼–4¾ in across. It retains its dome shape for some time before opening out fully. It is silky white, ageing to light brown. The stem is 1¼–4 in, white, tapering to the base,

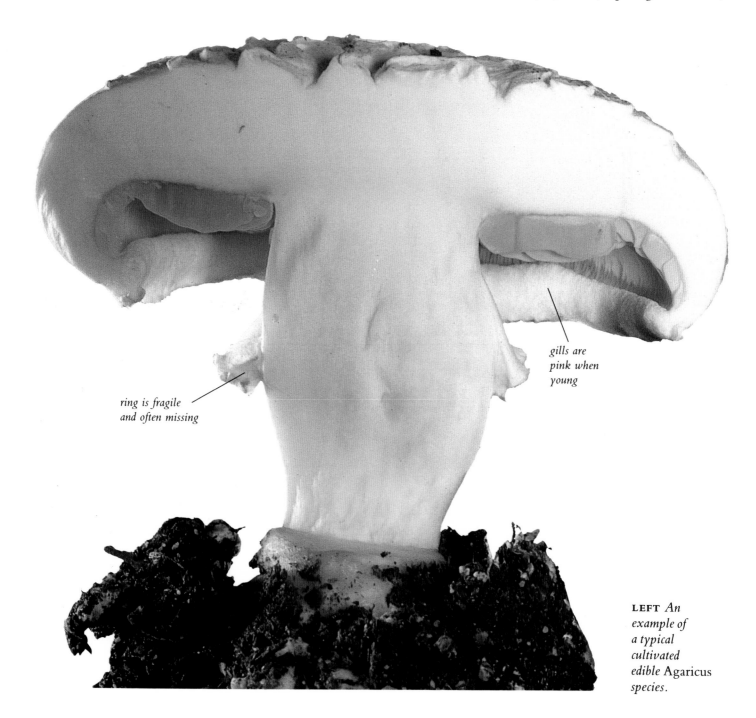

gills are
pink when
young

ring is fragile
and often missing

LEFT *An example of a typical cultivated edible* Agaricus *species.*

RIGHT *Note that the gills are not attached to the stem, this is common to all* Agaricus.

BELOW *The gills are brown in mature specimens.*

and has a thin ring which is often torn away. Even in unopened field mushrooms the gills are deep pink, an excellent identification feature. The white flesh bruises slightly pink. It has a pleasant smell. The spore print is brown.

HABITAT AND SEASON

Field mushrooms grow in mature pasture and often favor alkaline soils. They can grow any time from early summer through to late autumn.

STORAGE

An excellent mushroom for storing dried as it retains its flavor extremely well. The smaller specimens can be threaded on string and dried whole, but larger ones should be sliced.

PREPARATION AND COOKING HINTS

These do not need peeling, a wipe with a damp cloth is sufficient, but do check them carefully to make sure there is no insect infestation. The best way to do this is to trim the stem carefully and slice through the center – any insects will then be easy to see. The older specimens are best used for sauces and stews, as these give a quite intense, dark brown color to the dish. Young specimens can be used as you like. They are delicious on their own or for breakfast with bacon and eggs.

Agaricus macrosporus

This is quite a common autumn mushroom. It grows in rings and is extremely good to eat. Some care over identification is necessary, because it can look like the poisonous yellow stainer. However, the shape of the cap and, in particular, the smell are reliable aids to ensuring you have the right mushroom.

IDENTIFICATION
The domed cap is 3–4 in across. It is off-white with light brown scales. The scaly stem is 2–4 in long, off-white and quite thick, with a slightly pointed base. The gills are pale pink at first, turning darker brown with age. The flesh is white and has a fairly distinct smell of almonds. The spore print is brown.

HABITAT AND SEASON
Grows in rings in mature pastures that have not been treated with chemicals. The season is from late summer to autumn.

thick ring with scaly under-side

gills free from the stem

RIGHT *Often very large, the white cap may develop fine scales on the surface, as here.*

STORAGE
This mushroom is very good to eat. It is best dried for storage, but specimens can be quite large so it is important to slice them first.

PREPARATION AND COOKING HINTS
Clean the stem carefully and brush the cap: peeling is usually unnecessary. Check your specimens carefully, especially the larger ones, which may have become insect-infested.

Agaricus silvaticus

This is a mushroom of mainly coniferous woodland, which grows in the same places year after year. It is also extremely good to eat.

IDENTIFICATION

The cap is 2–4 in across, convex and covered with brown scales which give it an overall broken pattern. The stem is 2–3 in, whitish, but striated with brown markings; it has a brown ring. The gills are pale cream at first but turn quite red with age. The flesh is white and stains bright red when cut at the base or lengthwise. It has very little smell. The spore print is brown.

HABITAT AND SEASON

The usual habitat is coniferous woods and the season is from early summer to late autumn.

STORAGE

This mushroom has quite an intense flavor. It is best dried, but as it is often large, it should be sliced first.

PREPARATION AND COOKING HINTS

Because this mushroom grows mainly in coniferous woods, the top will need to be brushed and any pine needles removed. Cut off and discard the lower portion of the stem and slice. It will give a wonderful flavor to your dishes. It is also good on its own, lightly sautéed with a little butter and basil, and served on toast.

ring with small scale on underside

scaly cap surface scratches red

Agaricus silvicola
WOOD MUSHROOM

The wood mushroom has many similarities to the larger horse mushroom but, as the name suggests, it grows almost exclusively in woodland. Take care, however, not to confuse it with either the yellow stainer, *Agaricus xanthodermus*, or some of the deadly *Amanitas*. Check identifying features carefully. It does not grow out of a volval cup, so there will be no sign of one, and if you turn the mushroom over or cut it you will quite clearly see the identification features. If in any doubt, leave it alone.

IDENTIFICATION

The cap is between 2–4 in across, domed at first before opening out to be almost flat. It is a creamy yellow which darkens with age. The stem is 2–3 in, quite thin and with a clearly marked ring. The gills are mid-pink before turning dark brown. The flesh is white and has a distinct anise smell. The spore print is dark brown.

HABITAT AND SEASON

The wood mushroom is quite common in coniferous and deciduous woods. Its season is the autumn.

STORAGE

These mushrooms do not store well, so use and enjoy them as soon as possible after you have picked them.

PREPARATION AND
COOKING HINTS

The young specimens are particularly tasty. Try coating the caps of young mushrooms in seasoned flour, dipping them in a batter made with beer or ale and then deep frying them: delicious.

ABOVE *Always a graceful slender mushroom, the wood mushroom grows exclusively in woodlands.*

Aleuria aurantia
ORANGE PEEL FUNGUS

This wonderfully bright fungus has a nice taste and texture. It is a useful addition to all wild mushroom dishes.

IDENTIFICATION
The cap is small, just under ¼–2 in across; it is cup-shaped and becomes quite wavy at the edges. The inner surface is bright orange in color. The underside is much lighter and almost velvety to the touch.

HABITAT AND SEASON
The orange peel fungus grows in fairly large clumps on almost bare earth in light grassland, along roads and in lawns. It is quite common and the season is from autumn through to early winter.

STORAGE
Drying is the best method of storage.

PREPARATION AND COOKING HINTS
Apart from cleaning it carefully, the orange peel fungus needs very little done to it. It is fairly tough, so can be lightly rinsed in water, then sliced thinly and added to your wild mushroom dishes, to which it will add both flavor and color.

ABOVE RIGHT *Often growing in large clusters, the orange peel fungus prefers disturbed soils along paths and tracks.*

RIGHT *The inner surface (the hymenium) contains the spore-producing cells which are called asci.*

Armillaria mellea
HONEY MUSHROOM

The honey mushroom (*Armillaria mellea* and closely related species) is the dreaded enemy of the gardener. This mushroom grows from black cords known as rhizomorphs which can travel enormous distances. They kill the host tree and infect large areas of woodlands. It is, without doubt, the most dangerous of all the tree parasites, causing intensive rot and a very untimely death. If you find honey mushrooms growing in your garden get expert advice fast. However, honey mushrooms are extremely good to eat and grow in very large quantities during the autumn.

IDENTIFICATION
The cap can range from ¾–7¾ in across and is also variable in shape and color. It starts by being convex, then flattens and is centrally depressed. The color varies from almost honey to dark brown. The stem is 2–6 in and can vary quite considerably in width, sometimes being quite tuberous and at others very slender.

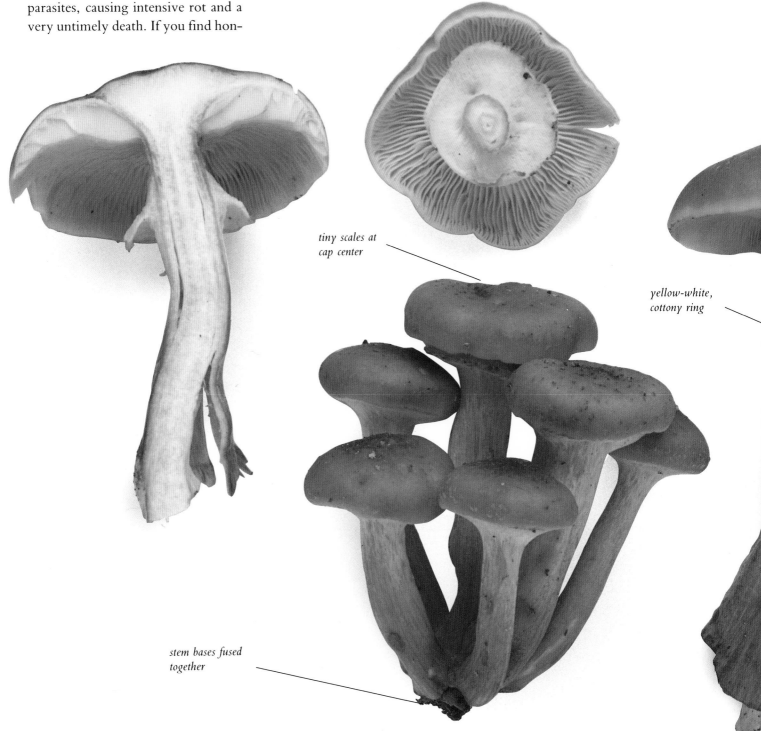

tiny scales at
cap center

yellow-white,
cottony ring

stem bases fused
together

The ring is always clearly visible. The gills vary from off-white to dark brown. The flesh is white with a smell that is quite strong and sweet. The spore print is off-white. It is now thought that there are five or six different forms of honey mushrooms. They usually grow in large clumps, either on dead tree trunks, tree stumps or living trees.

HABITAT AND SEASON

Honey mushrooms are fairly widespread in deciduous and coniferous woods, infecting living trees as well as dead trunks and stumps. The sea-

ABOVE *The scales of the cap vary considerably, ranging from almost smooth as seen here to quite coarse.*

BELOW *When old, the gills can be quite brownish but the spores are pale cream.*

son is from early summer to early winter and they can appear several times at the same place during a season.

STORAGE

Drying tends to toughen this mushroom, so it is best to make up dishes first and then freeze them.

PREPARATION AND
COOKING HINTS

Only the caps are edible – the stalks are very tough. If you have any allergic reaction, boil the caps for two or three minutes in lightly salted water, which must then be discarded as the mushroom may contain a mild toxin. Then cook as you wish. After the initial cooking the caps are particularly good sautéed lightly with onion, garlic and basil, thickened with a little cream and served with pasta.

Auricularia auricula

TREE EAR OR WOOD EAR

A common fungus with a very long growing season. It has some looka-likes, so take care with identification.

IDENTIFICATION

The fruit body of the tree ear is ¾–2¾ in across with a jelly-like texture and an ear-shaped appearance. In dry weather it becomes hard. It is tan-brown with small grayish hairs on the inner surface.

HABITAT AND SEASON

Grows on a wide variety of trees, sometimes on elder trees: it gets its old nickname Judas' Ear from Judas Iscariot who was said to have been hanged on an elder tree. It has an extremely long growing season and therefore can be collected throughout the year.

STORAGE

Best dried. In fact, if they are picked during dry weather when they are hard, they can be stored immediately. Before using, reconstitute by putting in lukewarm water.

PREPARATION AND COOKING HINTS

Wash thoroughly with several changes of water. As they have a gelatinous texture it is important to cook them well. A very nice way to serve them is to make a sauce with onions, garlic, basil and sliced tree ears, thickening it with a little cream, and using it to fill small patty shells or to spread on toast points.

velvety outer surface

inner surface appears smooth and rubbery

LEFT *If in doubt of your identification of this species, try stretching it between your fingers, it should be elastic and rubbery rather than brittle.*

BELOW *The color can vary greatly. These specimens are very young and fresh and so are quite pale: they may become quite purple-brown with age.*

Boletus badius
BAY BOLETE

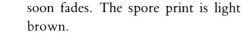

Bay boletus does not become infested with insects as much as some of the other boletes, but it is still best to pick only clean specimens. The flavor is excellent.

ABOVE *Bay boletes found under conifers (left) are usually darker, smoother and*

more maroon-bay in color than those found in deciduous wood (right).

IDENTIFICATION
The cap is 1½–7 in across, it is usually pale to mid-brown, although lighter specimens may be found. It has a polished appearance, and feels tacky when wet. The stem is 1¾–5 in and similar in color to the cap. The pores are light yellow, but stain blue if pressed or cut, which is one of the principal identification features of the bay boletes. The white flesh has a faint mushroomy smell, and also stains blue when cut, but the stain soon fades. The spore print is light brown.

HABITAT AND SEASON
In all types of mixed woodland. The season is early summer to late autumn.

STORAGE
A very versatile mushroom. Small specimens may be stored in jars of extra virgin oil, or in wine or cider vinegar. Larger specimens, however, are best sliced and dried after the

pores have been removed, because these will be quite wet and will not dry satisfactorily. These pores can be used in a mushroom sauce if you are making one at the time.

PREPARATION AND COOKING HINTS
Bay boletus are best picked when they are dry. Wipe the caps of any wet specimens and let them dry before dealing with them. However, fresh or dried, the bay bolete is very versatile and can be used in many wild mushroom dishes.

blue-grey stains when bruised

flesh may stain pale blue

no network on stem

Boletus chrysenteron
RED-CRACKED BOLETE

Although the flavor of this boletus is not as good as that of the bay boletes or the cep, young specimens are good in mixed mushroom dishes.

IDENTIFICATION

The cap is 1½–4 in across, light reddish-brown in color, but cracks in the surface of the cap often reveal a slightly reddish hue below. However, the red markings on the stem are the real giveaway of this bolete. The stem is 1½–3 in with a distinct reddish tinge for most of its length. The pores are yellow and much more open than those of the bay bolete; they stain a light greenish color. The flesh is cream to yellow and does not bruise on cutting. The spore print is light brown. The overall texture of this mushroom is much less dense than either the bay bolete or the cep.

HABITAT AND SEASON

Found in association with all broad-leaved trees. The season is throughout the autumn.

STORAGE

Dry this mushroom before adding it to your other dried mushrooms.

PREPARATION AND COOKING HINTS

Only pick young specimens, wipe or brush the cap to remove any loose particles of earth and slice thinly before cooking. However, because it can be a little mushy, it is best used in soups, stews and mixed dishes with other mushrooms and not on its own.

ABOVE *As the cap ages, particularly in colder weather, the entire surface may take on a reddish flush.*

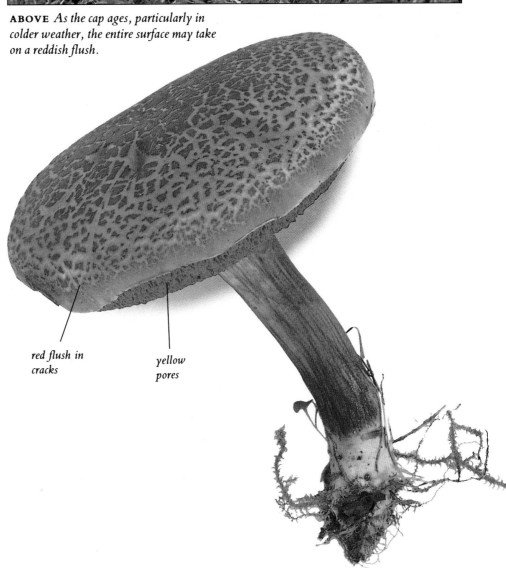

red flush in cracks

yellow pores

41

Boletus edulis
CEP OR PORCINI

Mushroom hunters regard this mushroom as a great prize; it has a wonderful nutty flavor and is extremely versatile. It can also grow very big and weigh as much as 2 lb 2 oz. It grows over a number of days and flies enter at the base of the stem and the insects work their way up to the cap and tubes so it is important to pick only those in prime condition. When collecting large specimens cut the cap in half to make sure there is no insect infestation before putting it in your basket.

IDENTIFICATION
The cap ranges from 2½–11¾ in across. Its light brown color looks rather like freshly baked bread. The color darkens as the cap opens, and it is at this stage that you should examine specimens for insect infestation. In wet weather the cap can have a slightly sticky appearance, but in dry weather it has a nice velvety sheen. The stem varies from 1¼–9 in. It is very bulbous and has a fine network, with markings that are more pronounced towards the cap.

yellow pores

white unchanging flesh

LEFT Ceps are a great culinary delicacy and they are considered at their best for eating when they are small and tight.

The pores are white at first, turning light yellow with age. The flesh is quite white and does not change as the mushroom ages. The spore print is light brown.

HABITAT AND SEASON
Coniferous, broad-leaved and mixed woodland; also beside grassy paths. It can also be found in association with heather, along with dwarf willows. The season is summer to late autumn and it is quite common.

RIGHT *A very variable species, some have swollen stems with much darker caps, particularly when found under conifers.*

white network on stem

STORAGE

Cut into thin slices this is probably the most important commercially dried mushroom in the world. Take your cue from this – drying is the best method of home storage. Small specimens can be kept in extra virgin olive oil, but it is really best to leave them so that they can grow on to more mature, and larger, specimens.

PREPARATION AND COOKING HINTS

Clean the caps well and cut in half to check for insects before putting them in the basket. Brush the stem, cutting off the bottom or scraping it to re-move any earth or fibers at the base. This is one of the most versatile mushrooms and it can be used in many cooked dishes.

Calocybe gambosa

St George's Mushroom

As its name suggests, St George's mushroom tends to appear around 23 April, St George's Day. It has a great variety of uses and is particularly welcome because it appears early in the year, at much the same time as the common morel. It frequently grows in rings which can be very large, although broken in places. The largest rings may be several hundred years old.

IDENTIFICATION

The cap is 2–6 in across with a slightly inrolled margin. Well rounded when young, large old specimens develop an irregular, wavy cap. It is white to cream in color. The stem is ¾–1½ in and white. The gills are narrow and crowded. The flesh is white and soft. It has a mealy smell which is pleasant and strong. The spore print is white.

HABITAT AND SEASON

Tends to grow in rings in grassy locations and around wood edges with underlying chalk. The season is from the beginning of April and into May. For good growth St George's mushroom relies on warmth and moisture so if the spring is cold it will not appear until the weather becomes warmer. Keep checking areas where you have seen it before.

RIGHT *The caps vary from white to a creamy yellow color.*

BOTTOM *In these mature specimens note how the caps are irregular and wavy.*

STORAGE

St George's mushroom dries extremely well. It can also be stored in virgin olive oil or in vinegar.

PREPARATION AND COOKING HINTS

Brush the caps well because they can be quite gritty and dirty and there may be chalk particles on the underneath. When picking this mushroom always cut the stem to avoid damaging the mycelial rings. It goes particularly well with chicken and fish. If you can get this mushroom, which is very rare in North America, try it in a chicken casserole.

Cantharellus cibarius
CHANTERELLE

The excitement of finding this mushroom is, for many, the highlight of the mushroom season – not only does it look beautiful, it tastes wonderful. Most collectors are secretive about their chanterelle patches because these mushrooms grow year after year, often in abundant quantities. It is, however, important to be sure you have found the true chanterelle and not simply the false chanterelle, *Hygrophoropsis aurantiaca*.

IDENTIFICATION
The cap is ¾–4¾ in across. Flat at first with a broken margin, it later becomes quite fluted with a central depression. The color can range from very pale to deep yellow, fading a little with age. Occasionally specimens are almost orange. The stem is 1¼–3 in, very solid and tapered towards the base. The yellow gills are blunt, narrow, irregular and run

cap depressed
when older

thick pale-yellow
flesh

blunt forking
gills or ridges

LEFT *The gills run down the stem and are the same color as the cap.*

down the stem. The yellowish flesh has a lovely faint fragrance of apricots – another important identification feature. The spore print is pale cream color.

HABITAT AND SEASON

In all kinds of woodland which have open mossy clearings. The season is early summer to late autumn.

STORAGE

All forms of storage can be recommended for the chanterelle. It is a particularly interesting one to store in spiced liquor because of its very fragrant flavor, but it is equally good stored in extra virgin olive oil or vinegar, or else dried.

PREPARATION AND
COOKING HINTS

It is important to clean chanterelles well when you pick them. Brush the caps, and wipe them with a damp cloth if necessary. Cut the stem to avoid any dirt getting into your basket. The chanterelle has a good shelf-life: specimens can be kept fresh for

some time either in a refrigerator or in a cool, airy place. They taste exquisite and are extremely versatile, whether on their own, in mixed mushroom dishes or with meat or fish dishes. They also give an elegant

color to sauces and the overall appearance of a dish. Try mixing all different types of *Cantharellus*: this will combine the different flavors and textures and make a brilliantly colorful dish of wild mushrooms.

LEFT *Observe how the gills of this species are very shallow, blunt and frequently forked, more like deep wrinkles or veins than true gills.*

Cantharellus infundibuliformis
WINTER CHANTERELLE

The winter chanterelle is so called because it usually appears much later than the ordinary chanterelle. It is quite an achievement to find these tiny little gems hidden under falling autumn leaves. But once you get your eye in, you will find groups of them growing where before you had hardly seen anything. They tend to grow in the same place each year, so note where you find them.

IDENTIFICATION
The cap is ¾–2 in across, convex at first, soon becoming funnel-shaped with a fluted edge. It is dark brown on top, very much the same color as the leaf cover under which it grows. The stem is 2–3 in, yellow and hollow. The gills are narrow and quite irregular, yellowish at first they are

grayish-lilac forked gills or wrinkles

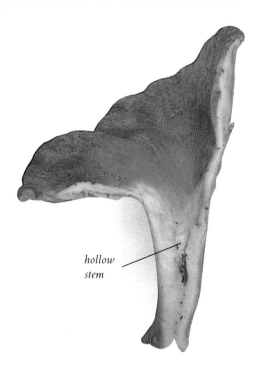

hollow stem

brown cap surface

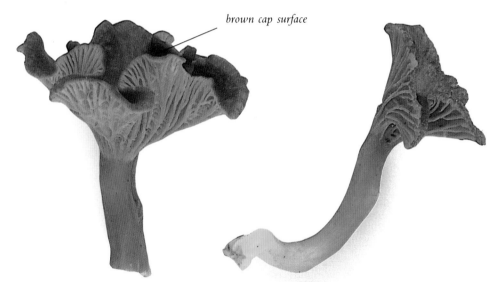

grayish lilac in older specimens. The flesh is yellowish and smells faintly sweet. The spore print is yellow.

HABITAT AND SEASON

Grows in large numbers in both deciduous and coniferous woods, preferring acid soil. The season is from late summer to late autumn.

STORAGE

Winter chanterelles dry extremely well, but can also be stored in extra virgin olive oil or wine vinegar.

PREPARATION AND COOKING HINTS

As these usually grow through leaf mold they are quite clean, so all they are likely to need is a dusting with your brush. And if you cut the stalks rather than pulling them up, you will avoid earth and other debris. They are very versatile in cooking, with an extremely nice, sweet flavor that goes especially well with fish.

ABOVE *A good tip for finding these mushrooms is to follow woodland streams and search on the mossy banks, as this is one of their favorite habitats.*

ABOVE *When growing in fallen leaves, winter chanterelles are very difficult to spot.*

Clitocybe odora
ANISE MUSHROOM

The aniseed toadstool is most useful as a condiment. Be careful when you identify it, because the verdigris agaric, *Stropharia aeruginosa*, looks rather similar, although it has a blunt knob at the center when open, and is always sticky and darkish-green in color. As the name suggests, the anise mushroom has a very pungent anise smell.

IDENTIFICATION

The cap is 1¼–2¾ in across; button-shaped at first, it soon flattens and sometimes becomes wavy. The color is a blue-green which darkens with

cap surface is dry, not sticky

gills are pale greenish-white

no ring on stem

RIGHT AND BELOW *This lookalike,*
Stropharia aeruginosa, *has a sticky cap
and a ring on the stem. It has no odor. The
gills turn purple-brown when mature.*

BOTTOM *The
color may fade
rapidly from that
shown to almost
white. These
specimens are best
avoided in case of
confusion with the
suspect* Clitocybe
fragrans, *which is
white and also
smells of anise.*

age. The stem is 1¼–2½ in and lightly striated. The gills, which are not very marked, are close and run down the stem. The flesh is pale and the smell is strongly of anise. The spore print is white.

HABITAT AND SEASON
In leaf mold along the edges of coniferous and deciduous woods. In the latter they are likely to be in association with beech or oak. The season is from late summer to late autumn and they are relatively common.

STORAGE
Best dried and stored separately because of the intensity of its flavor.

**PREPARATION AND
COOKING HINTS**
The anise mushroom is best used as a flavoring: finely chop fresh specimens or pulverize dried ones.

Coprinus comatus
SHAGGY INK CAP

One of the most common mushrooms, they often come up in dense clusters on newly turned earth in meadows and gardens throughout the summer. Only the young specimens are edible and once picked they must be used quickly, otherwise they soon decay into a nasty inky mass. This is an easy mushroom to identify as it is very distinct, although care must be taken that the early stages of this and the magpie fungus, *Coprinus picaceus*, are not mistaken. However, the magpie fungus has some veil-like patches covering the cap which the shaggy ink-cap does not.

IDENTIFICATION
The cap is 2–4¾ in across; egg-shaped at first, it opens into a bell. White with a cream-colored center; it has large shaggy scales. The stem is 4–14½ in and white. The gills are white to start with, slowly changing to black from the edge inwards before becoming a mass of ink which, incidentally, makes good drawing ink. The flesh is white with a slight sweet smell. The spore print is brown-black.

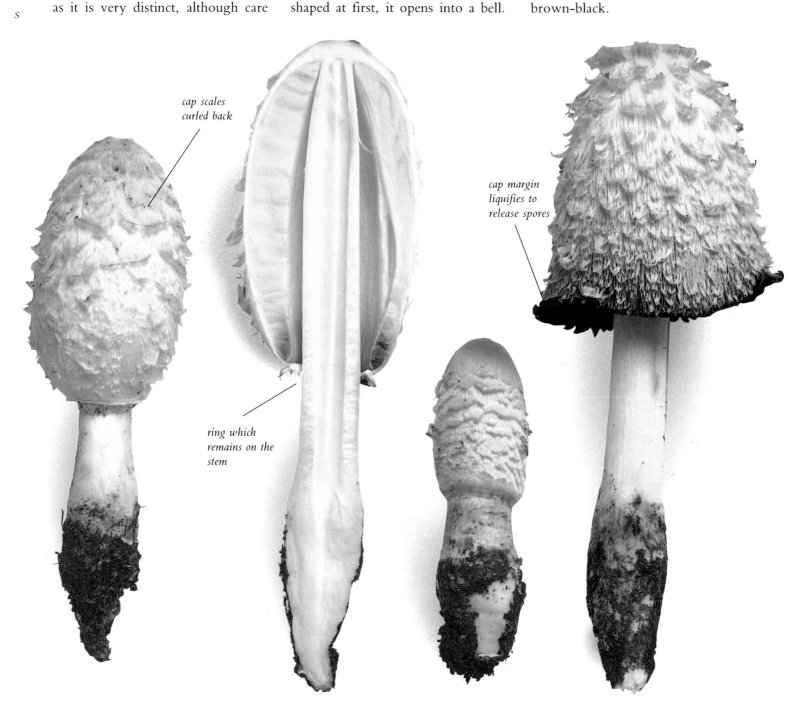

cap scales
curled back

ring which
remains on the
stem

cap margin
liquifies to
release spores

HABITAT AND SEASON

Widespread on grassy banks beside roads, on compost heaps, lawns and recently disturbed soil near building sites. The season is midsummer to late autumn. They are very common.

STORAGE

Best used fresh or dried in an electric drier. Do not attempt to air-dry them as they will turn into an inky mass.

PREPARATION AND
COOKING HINTS

Although shaggy ink caps can be used dried; they are really best fresh, either on their own, or with the parasol mushroom, *Macrolepiota procera*, to make a wonderful soup. Use the two mushrooms, some onions and a little potato to thicken, sweated together and then puréed. Simple and quite delicious.

BELOW *The very distinct narrow ring is not easily seen here, but as the cap expands it will be left behind on the stem.*

ABOVE *This is the best stage to collect shaggy ink caps for cooking.*

LEFT *Magpie fungus,* Coprinus picaceus *can be confused with the shaggy ink cap in its early stages.*

Craterellus cornucopioides
HORN OF PLENTY OR BLACK TRUMPETS

Another wonderful mushroom of the *Cantharellus* family. Like the chanterelle and winter chanterelle, the horn of plenty appears in large groups in the same place year after year. These, however, are quite often covered by dead leaves and are difficult to spot because of their color. Although the initial appearance is not inviting, the taste is excellent.

IDENTIFICATION

The cap is ¾–3½ in across; it is shaped like a tube or a trumpet and has an open flared mouth and is hollow. It becomes irregular with age and is thin and tough. In color it ranges from mid-brown to black, though it fades with age. The gills are barely perceptible. The flesh is grey to black. The spore print is white.

HABITAT AND SEASON

Grows in large clusters among the dead leaves of deciduous woods. The season is from late summer to quite late autumn.

STORAGE

All forms of storage are appropriate for the horn of plenty, but it is probably best dried.

trumpet-like depression

smooth to slightly wrinkled surface

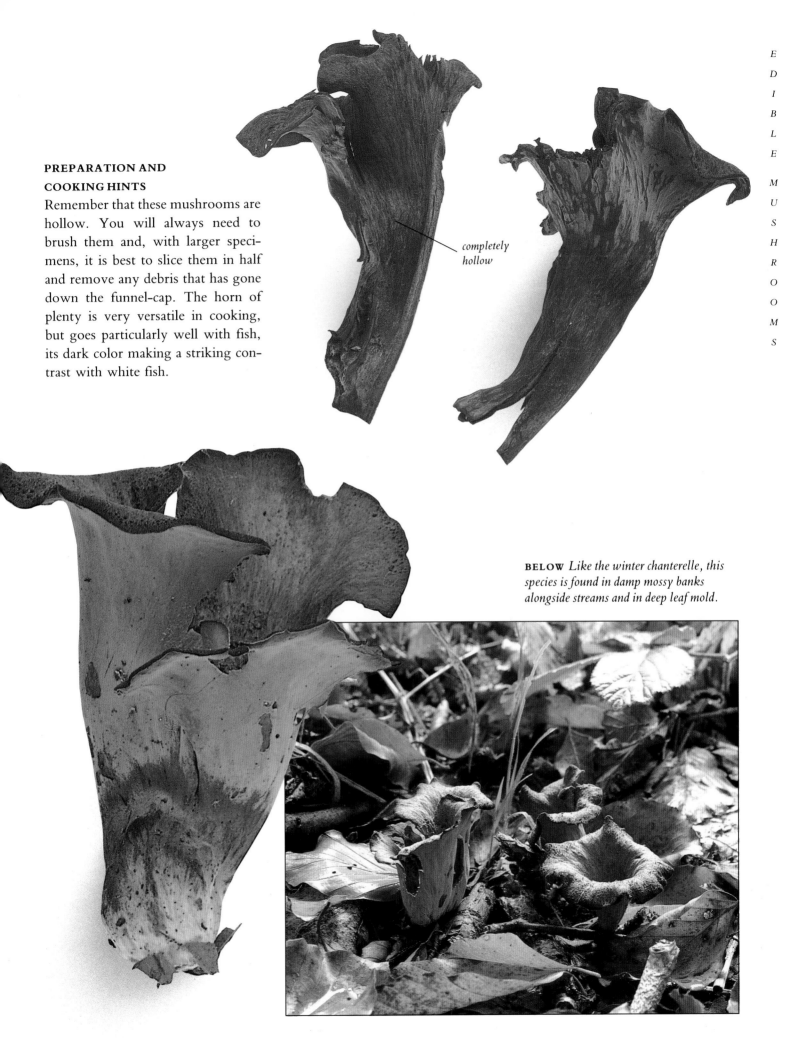

PREPARATION AND
COOKING HINTS

Remember that these mushrooms are hollow. You will always need to brush them and, with larger specimens, it is best to slice them in half and remove any debris that has gone down the funnel-cap. The horn of plenty is very versatile in cooking, but goes particularly well with fish, its dark color making a striking contrast with white fish.

completely
hollow

BELOW *Like the winter chanterelle, this species is found in damp mossy banks alongside streams and in deep leaf mold.*

Fistulina hepatica
BEEFSTEAK FUNGUS

An important bracket fungus from a collector's point of view, not only is it interesting in color and texture, it has a good flavor. Because the beef-steak fungus often grows fairly high up trees, you may well need to add a ladder to your collecting equipment.

IDENTIFICATION
The bracket can vary from 3–11¾ in across and is quite thick. It is usually in a single piece, although several may grow one above the other. Cut through, the beefsteak fungus really does look rather like a piece of meat. The color of the bracket is an orange-red darkening with age, the pores are much lighter. The flesh is thick, succulent and mottled dark red; it has quite a pleasant smell. The spore print is brown.

HABITAT AND SEASON
Grows on oak trees, usually, but not always, on the lower part of the trunk. Season is late summer to autumn, although it may appear earlier. Although this fungus causes rot inside a tree it does not kill it, but it makes the wood of infected trees much darker. Oak darkened in this way is in demand in the furniture

cut flesh
"bleeds" red juice

pores pull apart
very easily

industry. Near Holt, in north Norfolk, England, there is a 980-year-old oak tree with beefsteak fungus growing up to a height of 40 ft from the base, a little bit difficult from a picker's point of view, but nevertheless a wonderful sight.

STORAGE

Like other bracket fungi this will toughen if dried, so it is best to make dishes and then freeze them.

PREPARATION AND
COOKING HINTS

Cut off any parts of the tree still attached to the fungus. Separate the various layers and wipe them with a damp cloth. The beefsteak fungus has a slightly metallic taste, so it is best to slice it into strips and soak these in milk for about two hours to remove the slight acidity and acrid flavor. Then it can be broiled like a piece of steak with a little onion, basil and garlic. Try it, too, on a charcoal grill or barbecue. It is also excellent added to soups and stews for extra flavor and color.

Flammulina velutipes
VELVET SHANK

As the name implies, the velvet shank has a dark velvety stem. It normally grows during the winter months and can survive the frosts, indeed it may need a frost before starting to grow. It can be frozen solid, but still survive.

IDENTIFICATION
The cap is 1¼–4 in across and fairly flat. It is light orange in color, paler at the edges and darker towards the center. It is also quite smooth and shiny with a sticky surface. The stem is ½–1¼ in, very tough and is, as the name suggests, velvety and dark in color, particularly at the base. The flesh, which is yellow on the cap changing to dark brown on the stem, has little smell. The gills are pale yellow. The spore print is white.

HABITAT AND SEASON
The velvet shank often grows in very large clusters on dead or decaying wood, particularly in association with elm and oak. The season is long because they grow all through the winter months in more temperate zones and so are useful when only a limited number of mushrooms is available.

STORAGE
The best method of storage is to dry and pulverize them.

PREPARATION AND COOKING HINTS
As they have a fairly tough texture they really are best dried. If using them fresh, cut off most of the stem, and slice the caps finely. Use to give a good flavor to soups and stews, but remember to cook them well.

dense clusters of stems

black, velvety stem base

no ring on stem

LEFT *Difficult to confuse with anything else because of the unusual season of growth but note the absence of a ring on the stem. Poisonous lookalikes will have a ring or a veil.*

Grifola frondosa (syn. Polyporus frondosus)
HEN OF THE WOODS

BELOW AND BOTTOM *Look for small overlapping caps and flesh which does not turn brown when bruised.*

This is an unusual fungus which, like the cauliflower fungus, grows at the base of tree trunks and can be extremely large. Its many caps are joined together and a large specimen can provide a feast for many people. Good to eat and quite rare, so note where you find it as it will certainly grow there again.

IDENTIFICATION
The fruit body is 4–6¾ in across, and consists of a central section with many branch stems ending in individual caps. Each cap is 1¼–2¾ in across and has quite a wrinkled edge. The whole fruit body is grayish in color turning brown with age. The stems are pale gray. The hen of the woods has tubes rather than gills. These are ¹⁄₁₀ in long and run down the stem. The flesh, which is white, has a slightly musty smell.

HABITAT AND SEASON
Hen of the woods grows at the base of the trunks of oaks or other deciduous trees. Occasionally it grows on tree stumps. The season is autumn to early winter.

STORAGE
The best method of storage is drying. Otherwise freeze dishes in which you have used this mushroom.

PREPARATION AND COOKING HINTS
It is important to clean the hen of the woods thoroughly as it has many nooks and crevices which harbor dirt. Due to its very tough texture it can be rinsed in cold water prior to cooking. It tastes good and goes well in a wide variety of wild mushroom dishes, but, because of its tough texture, make sure it is well cooked. Dried and then powdered, it can be added to soups and stews.

Hydnum repandum
HEDGEHOG FUNGUS

This little gem is often quite difficult to find on the woodland floor. Perseverance pays as it has great culinary value and is much sought after by collectors.

IDENTIFICATION
The cream-colored caps are usually single and ¾–6 in across, flattening with a slight central depression and rolled rim. The stem is 1¾–3 in and quite bulbous. It is quite downy, and is white, bruising slightly yellow when cut. In place of pores or veins, this mushroom has little spines, hence the name hedgehog fungus. The flesh is white with a very pleasant smell. The spore print is cream-colored.

HABITAT AND SEASON
Grows in large numbers and under deciduous or coniferous trees, usually in quite damp sites such as along drainage ditches or where there are mossy patches. The season is late summer to late autumn.

STORAGE
These are best sliced and dried for winter use, although they can be kept in oil or vinegar.

PREPARATION AND COOKING HINTS
After cleaning, the smaller specimens can be cooked whole or else sliced. With larger specimens it is probably best to remove the spines, as although quite edible they look like small hairs and could spoil the appearance of the finished dish. This is a very versatile mushroom, going very well with both meat and fish dishes, but it is worth trying some on their own for their excellent flavor.

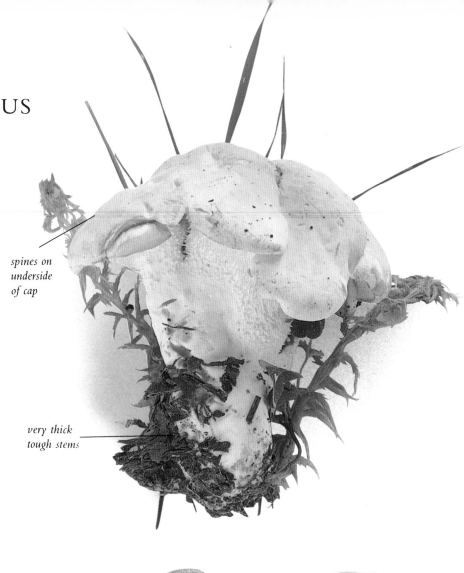

spines on underside of cap

very thick tough stems

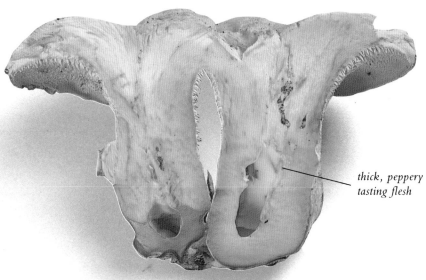

thick, peppery tasting flesh

LEFT *The cap color can vary from pinkish-buff to this rare white form.*

Hypholoma sublateritium
BRICK CAP

These small mushrooms, which appear in clusters in the autumn, are good to eat. However, it is quite easy to confuse them with the sulphur tuft, *Hypholoma fasciculare*, which is poisonous, so it is important to take care when identifying them.

IDENTIFICATION
The cap is 1½–4 in across and quite convex, although it can flatten in mature specimens. As the name suggests, the cap is brick red, darkest in the center and often paler towards the margins. The stem is 2–7 in long and whitish, but can stain darker when cut. It has a partial veil. The gills are purplish-gray. The flesh is pale yellow and slightly darker towards the

BELOW *Note the veil remnants on the cap margin and the robust, fleshy caps and stems. These specimens are unusually wet and sticky.*

stem. It has a definite smell of mushrooms. The spore print is purple-brown.

HABITAT AND SEASON
The brick cap grows in clusters on the stumps of old deciduous trees, from late autumn to early winter.

STORAGE
Only keep the caps, which are best dried whole for storage.

PREPARATION AND COOKING HINTS
Only collect the young specimens when they are at their very best. Cooked lightly these give a good flavor to any dish.

BOTTOM *Note how the gills flush purple as the spores mature. They are never greenish-yellow like the sulphur tuft.*

61

Laccaria amethystea
AMETHYST DECEIVER

The amethyst deceiver grows in large groups. It is colorful, edible and tasty, and so makes excellent additions to your cooking.

IDENTIFICATION
The cap is ½–2 in across. It is convex but flattens with age and develops a slight depression in the center. Deep purplish-lilac in color, it dries to an almost buff color. The stem is 1½–4 in, hollow and has slightly white fibers below the cap. The gills are a similar color to the cap. The flesh is thin and tinged lilac. The smell is not distinctive. The spore print is white.

HABITAT AND SEASON
Grows in coniferous and deciduous woods, often with beech. The season is late summer to early winter. It is very common.

STORAGE
Dries very well. It can also be stored in spiced liquor to give a most unusual sauce to serve over ice cream and desserts.

PREPARATION AND COOKING HINTS
As these grow quite densely and have wide open gills, they can be dirty, so it is important to clean them well before using. If you store them in spiced liquor, blanch them first. It is important that if stored in liquor these are kept in a refrigerator to prevent fermentation. They are also excellent fresh.

cap becomes much paler when dry

LEFT *When picked, amethyst deceivers are bright in color but this will fade.*

Laccaria laccata
DECEIVER

Like the amethyst deceiver, the deceiver grows in large groups.

IDENTIFICATION
The deceiver has a cap that can be slightly larger than the amethyst deceiver, but is also convex and flattening. It can open to look like a chanterelle. The color is tawny to pale red and it dries to a paler color. The stem is 2–4 in, a similar color to the cap, but often is twisted. The gills are well spread. The flesh is a pale reddish-brown and the smell is not distinctive. The spore print is white.

HABITAT AND SEASON
Grows in coniferous and deciduous woods. The season is late summer to early winter. They are very common.

STORAGE
The best method of storage is drying.

PREPARATION AND COOKING HINTS
Like the amethyst deceiver, it is important to clean it well before putting it in your basket. Follow the instructions on the opposite page for spicing in liquor.

RIGHT ABOVE AND BELOW *The deceiver is incredibly variable and it may take you many seasons to recognize the many variations.*

Lactarius deliciosus
Saffron Milk-cap

A lovely, colorful mushroom to find. It grows very close to the ground and often on quite sandy soil, which can make cleaning difficult. It also has a hollow stem which can lead to problems with infestation. To avoid this problem just pick young fresh specimens, but at the same time make sure that they are mature enough for a positive identification, otherwise they can be confused with the woolly milk-cap, *Lactarius torminosus*, or *Lactarius pubescens*, both of which are poisonous.

IDENTIFICATION

The cap is 1¼–4¾ in across, convex with a depressed center. It has concentric rings and, as the name suggests, is saffron in color. On cutting

ABOVE *As you can see, the cap becomes pale, almost silvery-white or dull greenish with age. Pick the fresher orange caps.*

cap with
concentric rings

stains green
when bruised

bleeds orange
milk when cut

you will notice that it bleeds a saffron color. It also has a clean, inrolled edge. This is an important means of identification, because neither the woolly milk-cap nor *Lactarius pubescens* have clean edges to the cap. The hollow stem is 1¼–2½ in pale, blotched with orange, and when bruised or broken, turns greenish. The closely spaced gills are saffron in color. The flesh is pale. The saffron milk-cap is brighter in color than either of its lookalikes, which is a useful aid to identification.

HABITAT AND SEASON

Always grows under pine or spruce trees, and can also be found beside paths on sandy terrain. The season is early summer to quite late autumn.

STORAGE

This stores extremely well, whether dried or in oil or vinegar.

PREPARATION AND
COOKING HINTS

The sand and pine needles of this mushroom's habitat make cleaning important. Indeed, it may be necessary to wash your specimens immediately before cooking, but then dry them well before slicing and cooking them. The lovely crunchy texture and good flavor make this a much sought-after mushroom.

BELOW *In young specimens the margin is involuted.*

RIGHT *The cap margin is shaggy in these young specimens.*

Laetiporus sulphureus
SULPHUR POLYPORE OR CHICKEN OF THE WOODS

One of the more spectacular of all bracket fungi, this can grow in very large quantities and come quite early in the mushroom season. Its versatility makes it important from a culinary point of view, but only pick young specimens.

IDENTIFICATION
The bracket can range from 6–19¾ in across. Often the shape of a fan, it has a semi-circular growing habit and softly rounded edges. The color is spectacular; lemon to orange-yellow, although it tends to darken with age. The brackets have an almost velvet-like appearance. It has yellow tubes. The flesh in young specimens is tender and exudes a yellow juice. The smell is quite pungent and a little acrid.

HABITAT AND SEASON
Grows on deciduous trees, particularly oak but may also be found on yew, cherry and willow. The season is usually from late spring to early autumn, but if the winter has been mild it will often appear much earlier depending on the zone, so keep a look out for it.

STORAGE
Drying toughens this mushroom, so it is best used fresh and the finished dish frozen.

PREPARATION AND COOKING HINTS
Avoid the toughest specimens and only use young ones. Cleaning can be difficult but it is best to separate the individual layers, brushing lightly; bearing in mind that the dense texture makes it possible to wash it to remove any infestation or dirt. If you notice a slight bitter taste blanch it for two to three minutes in boiling, salted water prior to cooking. The texture and flavor is of chicken, as the name suggests, and it is much prized by chefs. It is wonderful for vegetarian meals, making an excellent chicken of the woods risotto or chicken of the woods curry.

BELOW *The giant polypore, Meripilus giganteus, can reach 3 ft across. Its flesh stains black when bruised but it is edible when very young.*

BELOW LEFT OPPOSITE AND BELOW *When young, the strange lumpy growths of Laetiporus sulphureus look quite unlike the elegant brackets it will form with age.*

BOTTOM *This bracket lasts quite a while in the field and when old is soft, spongy and paler in color. Pick brightly colored fruit bodies.*

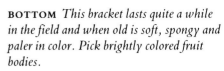

Langermannia gigantea
GIANT PUFFBALL

The giant puffball can be truly spectacular. It is also versatile in the kitchen, but only pick specimens that are fresh and young and sound hollow when you tap the top of the mushroom. It is pointless picking this mushroom once the flesh has become discolored. Check its age by cutting the specimen right through; the knife should not tear the flesh but pass crisply through it.

IDENTIFICATION
The fruit body can range from 2–31½ in across, although specimens of 48 in across have been recorded. When young it has a clean white appearance, although the outer wall may break away to expose the spore mass and become yellow. Avoid at this stage.

LEFT *Hedges and ditch banks are the favorite habitats of the giant puffball.*

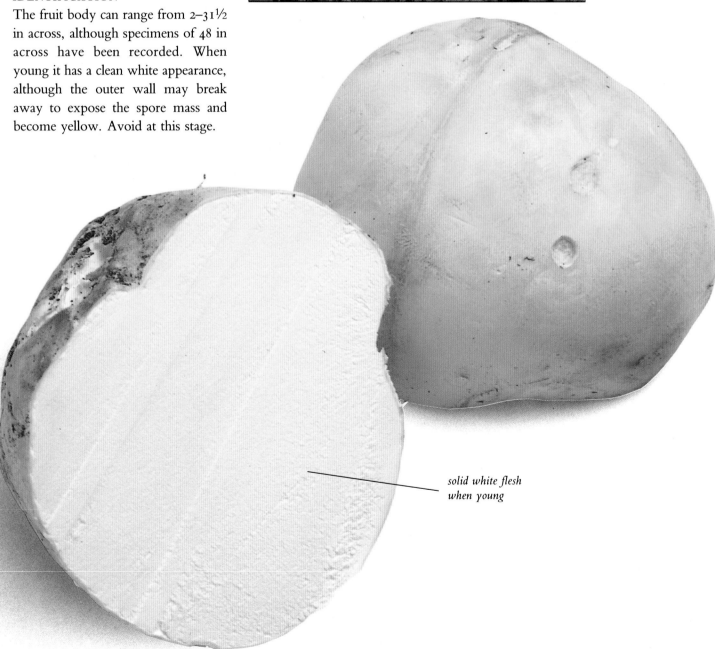

solid white flesh when young

HABITAT AND SEASON

The giant puffball grows in gardens, pastures, woodlands and a wide variety of other situations, such as along stream banks. The season is any time from early summer to late autumn unless the weather is very dry, when it will not grow. There will usually be several in the same area and they grow in the same place year after year after year.

STORAGE

There is no satisfactory way of storing giant puffballs, so it is best to make up the dishes and freeze them.

PREPARATION AND
COOKING HINTS

Very little needs to be done to this mushroom. Wipe the specimens carefully with a damp cloth and, if you are not going to use them immediately, wrap in a paper bag and keep in the refrigerator for up to three days. The giant puffball goes extremely well in all wild mushroom dishes, soups and stews. It also makes a good breakfast sliced and fried with bacon or else dipped in beaten egg and breadcrumbs and lightly fried in bacon fat or corn oil.

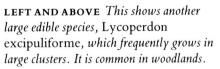

LEFT AND ABOVE *This shows another large edible species,* Lycoperdon excipuliforme, *which frequently grows in large clusters. It is common in woodlands.*

Leccinum scabrum
BROWN BIRCH BOLETE

Although the brown birch bolete is not as well favored as the orange birch bolete, it is still quite useful in the kitchen. However, only pick young firm specimens as older ones tend to absorb a good deal of moisture and so have a very soft texture.

IDENTIFICATION

The cap is 2–4¾ in across and mid-brown in color. It is dry, but can be slightly sticky in wet weather. The stem is 2¾–7¾ in, white with brown to blackish flecked scales. The pores are brown. The flesh is white and the smell quite pleasant. The spore print is brown.

HABITAT AND SEASON

Grows under birch trees. The season is summer to late autumn.

STORAGE

Drying is the best method of storage. Cut it into sections and either air-dry or use an electric dryer.

PREPARATION AND COOKING HINTS

As this mushroom has quite a soft texture, it is best to use it in conjunction with other mushrooms in a mixed mushroom dish or in mushroom soups.

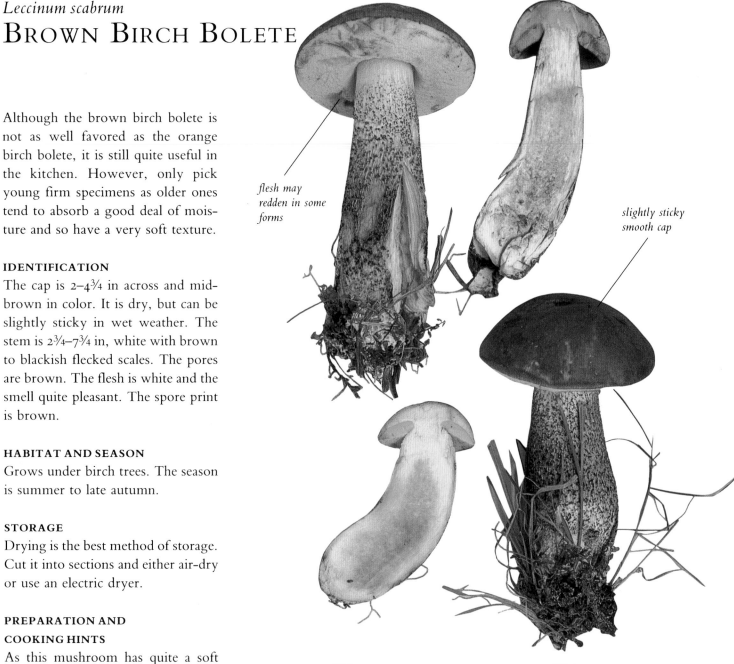

flesh may redden in some forms

slightly sticky smooth cap

RIGHT *The brown birch bolete has recently been subdivided into a number of closely related species, all of which are edible.*

Leccinum versipelle
ORANGE BIRCH BOLETE

A bolete that is particularly good to eat. It can grow to a fairly large size and, as the name implies, is usually in close association with birch trees.

IDENTIFICATION

The cap is 2½–9¾ in across. It is a lovely orange color and has a slightly fluffy appearance at first before becoming smooth or scaly, depending on the weather conditions. It is usually dry. The stem can be up to 7¾ in. It is white to grayish in color and covered with brown to blackish scales. The stems of young specimens bruise a bright electric blue in patches. The pores are off-white to gray. The flesh is pale, becoming blackish with age. The smell is quite pleasant. When cut in cross-section this mushroom stains quite black on the inside, but you should not be put off by this as it is good to eat. The spore print is light brown.

HABITAT AND SEASON

Grows in association with birch and scrub. The season is midsummer to quite late autumn.

STORAGE

Because this mushroom can be quite large, it is best to slice it before drying, which is the best way of storing it.

PREPARATION AND COOKING HINTS

It should only be necessary to wipe the cap with a damp cloth and brush any loose dust particles from the stem. A versatile mushroom, it is much sought after by chefs.

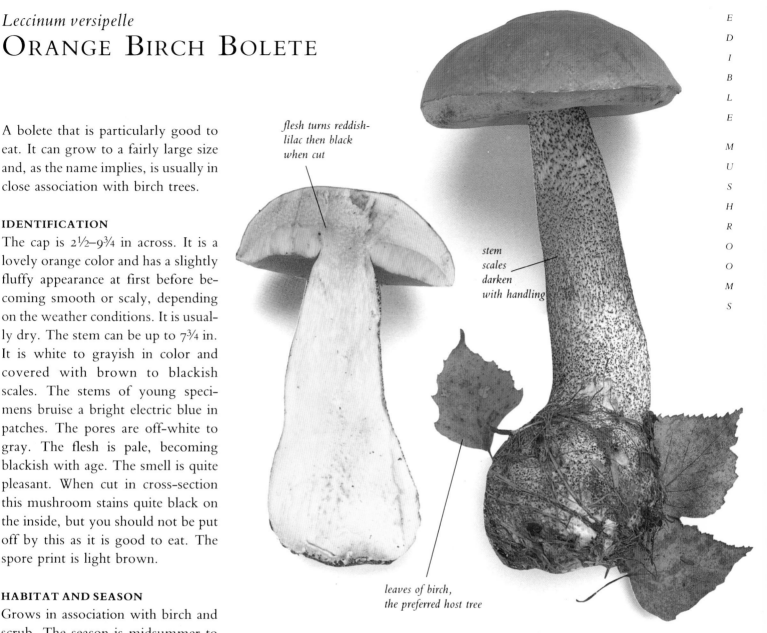

flesh turns reddish-lilac then black when cut

stem scales darken with handling

leaves of birch, the preferred host tree

ABOVE *The caps may expand to a much greater size in proportion to the stem than is shown here and the color can fade to dull yellow buff.*

ABOVE *The cap may become quite felt-like and scaly with age, particularly at the center.*

Lepista nuda (syn. *Clitocybe nuda*)
WOOD BLEWIT

The wood blewit is useful because it appears late in the season. But beware – some people are allergic to it. Make sure you try only a little first and take care if you serve it to guests. It is also most important to remember it must be well cooked and never eaten raw.

IDENTIFICATION

The cap is 2½–4¾ in across. Convex at first, it eventually flattens and is sometimes quite irregular. The cap starts by being quite blue but then turns an almost shiny tan. It dries a little paler. The stem is 2–3½ in and often has purple markings. The gills are crowded and very lilac, although they lose their color with age they never turn brown. It is best to pick younger specimens that still retain the wonderful color for they have the best flavor. The flesh is bluish and the smell is quite perfumed. The spore print is pale pink.

gills remain violet, never turn brown

smooth cap surface

tough, fibrous stem

HABITAT AND SEASON

Grows in all mixed woodland, hedges and gardens and sometimes on open ground. The season is from autumn to early winter. It is quite common and often grows in large quantities.

STORAGE

Because the wood blewit must be cooked before it is eaten, it is best not to dry it. It does, however, keep extremely well if it is blanched and then put in wine vinegar, extra virgin olive oil or spiced liquor. But, if kept in the liquor, it must be stored in the refrigerator to stop fermentation. The color and fragrance of this mushroom mean it can be used in both sweet and savory dishes.

PREPARATION AND COOKING HINTS

Quite an easy mushroom to clean, gently wipe the top and cut the stem. It is good in all mushroom dishes, but as it has a very strong flavor it goes particularly well with strongly flavored vegetables such as onions and leeks. Try a blewit bake by mixing onions, leeks and wood blewits in a béchamel sauce. Do not forget, however, that some people are allergic to it.

TOP *Note that the caps are smooth and not sticky. The gills remain violet, never turning rusty brown as do those of some lookalike species, such as* Cortinarius.

RIGHT *Although these specimens are under pines, the blewit is equally common in deciduous woods and gardens.*

Lepista saeva
FIELD BLEWIT OR BLUE LEG

The field blewit is most commonly found exactly where the name suggests. But, because they are low-growing, they are difficult to spot in long grass. Its other name, blue leg, comes from the brightly colored stem. It is best picked young, to avoid infestation with insects. Remember, like the wood blewit, this mushroom must be cooked before it is eaten and some people are allergic to it, so take care.

IDENTIFICATION
The cap is 2½–4¾ in across. Quite convex at first, then flattening, it can be slightly depressed when fully

these are in perfect condition for picking

opened out. The cap is a rather insignificant buff color, but it has a nice shine. The stem, which is 1¼–2½ in is the most significant thing about the field blewit. It is often rather bulbous and has lilac markings. The gills are crowded and whitish. The flesh is quite thick and chunky and white to flesh-colored. It has a perfumed smell very similar to that of the wood blewit. The spore print is pale pink.

HABITAT AND SEASON
Often grows in large numbers in rings in pastures. The season is autumn through to the first frosts of

winter, although it can stand some light frosts.

STORAGE

As this is another mushroom that must be cooked before it is eaten, it is best blanched and stored in wine vinegar or extra virgin olive oil. Store in spiced liquor if you want to serve it as a dessert.

PREPARATION AND COOKING HINTS

Very similar to the wood blewit, the field blewit gives a really good flavor to stews if it is chopped up first.

ABOVE *Here, you can see clearly the complete lack of violet color in the cap, compared to the wood blewit.*

no violet in gills

bluish-lilac stem may fade when old

Macrolepiota procera

PARASOL MUSHROOM

The parasol mushroom can grow quite large and has a long growing season. They reappear in the same place year after year, and may well have several fruitings during the season. The name is appropriate, as this mushroom does indeed look like a lady's parasol.

IDENTIFICATION

The cap, which is 4–9¾ in or more, starts by being spherical, but soon flattens out, though retaining a prominent center. It is pale buff in color and covered with symmetrical patterns of dark shaggy scales. The stem is 6–11¾ in, white and has a large ring. The gills are white, becoming darker in age but never turning green. The flesh is thin and white and has a fairly sweet, although not particularly distinctive, smell. The spore print is white. This mushroom is usually insect-free and is best collected when dry as it soon absorbs moisture, becoming soggy and almost unusable.

HABITAT AND SEASON

In open woods and pastures, and along roadside hedges. The season of the parasol mushroom is from early summer to late autumn.

STORAGE

This mushroom dries well. Discard the stems, which are tough, cut the cap into segments and dry.

PREPARATION AND COOKING HINTS

This mushroom is usually clean and insect-free, so very little attention needs to be paid to cleaning. However, dust off any particles on the top, remove the stalk right into the cap and cut into segments. An excellent, if unusual, way of using it is to make up a batter with beer or ale instead of milk, dipping the pieces into the batter and then deep-frying them. Alternatively, you can dust the segments of cap in seasoned flour and shallow- or deep-fry. Cooked like this it makes a crisp start to a meal or a good addition to a main course.

Macrolepiota rhacodes
SHAGGY PARASOL

very
coarse
recurved
scales

The shaggy parasol is smaller than the parasol mushroom. Although it is edible it can cause stomach upsets, so serve to knowledgeable guests.

IDENTIFICATION

The cap is 2–4¾ in across; ovate at first, it expands to become almost flat. It gets its name from the cap's shaggy appearance. The markings are not as clear as those of the parasol, but it has quite a fibrous appearance. The stem is 4–6 in, off-white with a pinky-brown tinge. The gills are white at first, becoming tinged with red as it ages. The white-tinged flesh bruises reddish-brown or pink. When cut it turns red. The smell is aromatic. The spore print is white.

HABITAT AND SEASON

Grows in woods and shrubberies of all kinds, often with conifers as well as under hedges and along grassy roadsides. The season is early summer to late autumn.

STORAGE

A mushroom that dries extremely well. Discard the stalk, cut the cap into sections and dry. Reconstituted, it is excellent in soups and stews or mixed wild mushroom dishes.

PREPARATION AND COOKING HINTS

Very similar to the parasol. The shaggy parasol has a clean cap which needs very little attention other than a light brushing. If using fresh specimens, discard the stalk and cut the cap into segments, then deep fry or add to mushroom dishes. The smaller caps are good for stuffing.

ABOVE *The form shown here is the typical woodland type with dull-brown colors. In gardens a larger white form with very bulbous stem base occurs.*

stem ages and stains brown

ring will be left around stem

LEFT *The stems may be deep in leaf cover so look out for the bulbous base, which is a characteristic feature.*

77

Marasmius oreades
FAIRY RING MUSHROOM

One of the first mushrooms to appear in spring, the fairy ring mushroom tastes just as good as it looks. But beware, there is a poisonous look-alike, the *Clitocybe dealbata*, that grows in a very similar way in very similar sites. It is most important to learn to identify these two. There is very little similarity once they are full grown, but it is important not to make any mistakes.

IDENTIFICATION

The cap is ¾–2 in across, convex at first, then flattening with quite a marked center. Tan in color, it dries to a fairly light buff. The stem is ¾–4 in and tough, so it is best when picking to remove the stem entirely. The gills are white to tan and quite distant. The flesh is thick. The spore print is white.

HABITAT AND SEASON

It forms rings in the shorter grass of old pastures or lawns. The season is from late spring to late autumn. It is very common. It is essential to be able to distinguish between this mushroom and *Clitocybe dealbata*. The latter also grows in rings, often very close, within a meter, to those of the fairy ring mushroom. The color and gills are quite different and *Clitocybe*

dealbata does not appear so early in the year, but it is most important that you can identify them.

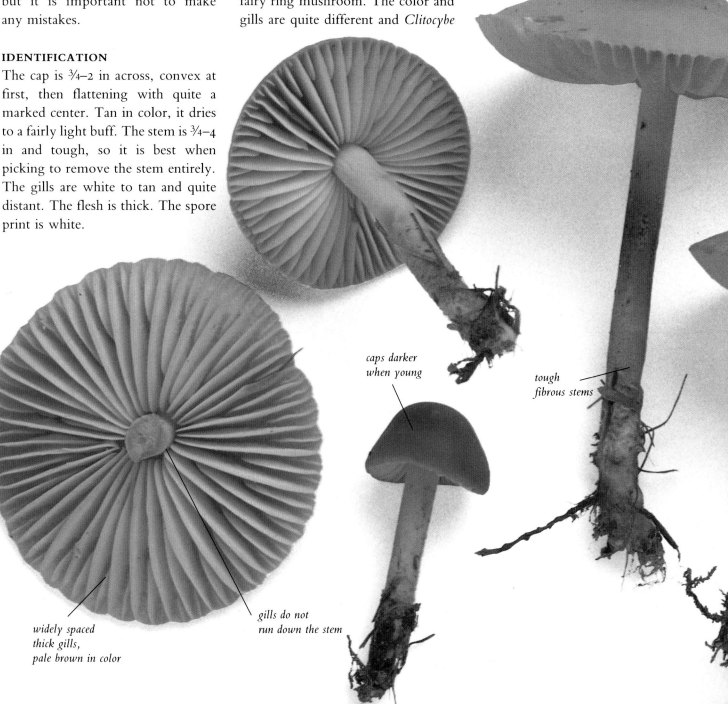

caps darker
when young

tough
fibrous stems

widely spaced
thick gills,
pale brown in color

gills do not
run down the stem

LEFT *This classic fairy ring is a few yards across, but they may reach over a hundred yards!*

STORAGE

These mushrooms are wonderful eaten fresh, but also dry very well. They can also be stored in spiced red Vermouth, extra virgin olive oil or wine or cider vinegar after blanching.

PREPARATION AND
COOKING HINTS

As long as you pick these mushrooms clean and cut off the stems when picking them from grass, the only problem you are likely to have is removing a few blades of grass. Occasionally a light dusting with a brush may be necessary, but washing definitely spoils the flavor. From a culinary point of view this is a versatile mushroom, going extremely well with meat and fish dishes as well as mixed mushroom dishes.

BELOW *Note how the grass is shorter where the mushrooms are growing because the nutrients have been absorbed by the fungi.*

Morchella elata
BLACK MOREL

A member of the highly edible morel family. This, like *Morchella esculenta*, grows in the early spring, so keep an eye open for it as soon as spring arrives.

IDENTIFICATION
Morchella elata is very similar to *M. esculenta* but much darker, often almost black with the ridges and pits aligned in vertical rows. The cap is often tall and pointed. The mushroom stands 2–6 in high.

HABITAT AND SEASON
Grows in gardens, waste ground, along roadsides and disused railway lines. Season is throughout the spring.

STORAGE
Like *M. esculenta*, the black morel is best dried.

PREPARATION AND COOKING HINTS
Clean thoroughly before cooking, slicing the fruit body in half to make sure it is free of insects. Cook and serve as you would *M. esculenta* and, like that morel, it must be properly cooked before it is eaten.

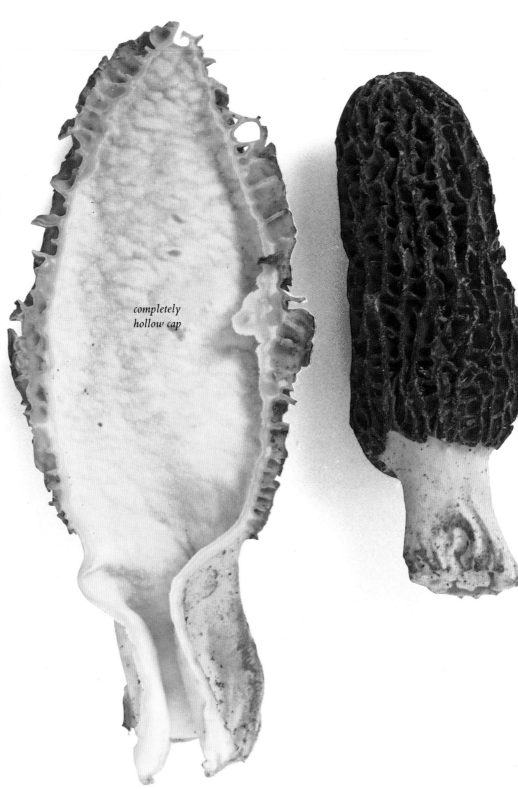

completely hollow cap

BELOW LEFT AND RIGHT *Another similar morel is the common morel,* Morchella vulgaris. *Look closely at these two examples, their caps may be dark but they have completely irregular pits and ridges unlike the black morels.*

RIGHT *Often occuring in large numbers, the black morel may be found in both deciduous and coniferous woodlands as well as along paths and in gardens.*

Morchella esculenta

The morels are among the most exciting springtime fungi. Careful examination of their habitat is necessary because they blend into their background so well. They usually grow singly; two or three can sometimes be found within a reasonably small area, but very rarely more. Excellent mushrooms from the culinary point of view, they must be cooked before eating – never, ever, eat them raw.

IDENTIFICATION
The fruit body is 2–7¾ in high. Although very convoluted, with a honeycomb effect, the overall shape is pointed. It is palish brown in color and darkens to orange-yellow with age. Inside it is hollow. The flesh is white to cream.

HABITAT AND SEASON
Found among shrubs or in open woodland, on waste ground, along path edges and often along disused railway lines. The season is throughout the spring. Wind is very important in spreading the spore of this fungus so, if you find a good specimen, follow the direction of the prevailing wind and you will often find some more.

STORAGE
Best dried for storage. Because of all the nooks and crannies, this morel is often infested with woodlice and other insects so will need cleaning thoroughly before drying and storing.

PREPARATION AND COOKING HINTS
The easiest way to clean this mushroom properly is to slice each one in half to make sure there is nothing hiding inside, rinse it in clear water and dry. One of the nicest ways to use fresh morels is to stuff the large fruit body. They also go well with meat dishes and provide a very rich sauce. Dried, the intensity of their flavor will enhance most wild mushroom dishes.

ABOVE *When young, the fruit body is often dull buff or brown in color with blunt ridges.*

ABOVE *When mature, the color changes to ochre or orange-yellow and the ridges become sharper.*

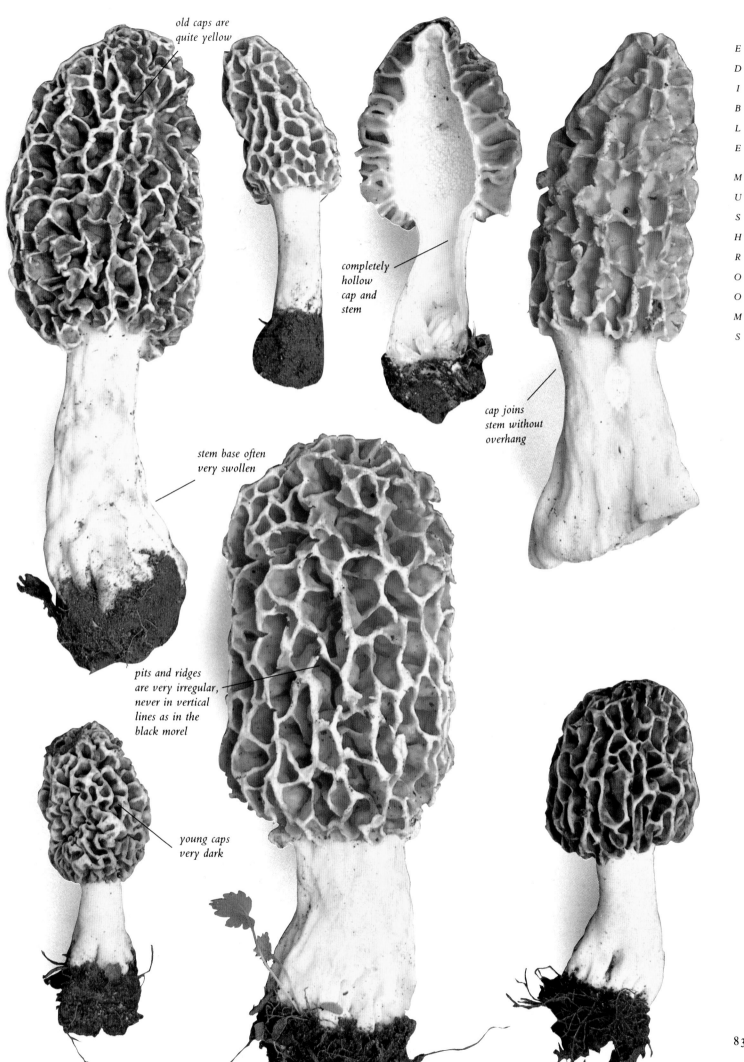

old caps are
quite yellow

completely
hollow
cap and
stem

cap joins
stem without
overhang

stem base often
very swollen

pits and ridges
are very irregular,
never in vertical
lines as in the
black morel

young caps
very dark

Pleurotus cornucopiae

BELOW *The stems here are shorter than usual for they often reach 2–3 in in length. The way that the stems are fused together is quite characteristic.*

This member of the oyster mushroom family is fairly widely spread. It can be found on the same trees and at the same time as the oyster mushroom, so always have a good look for it before you leave the tree.

IDENTIFICATION

The cap is 2–4¾ in across and convex. It often makes quite a funnel-like shape, which frequently becomes fluted and split at the edges. Whitish in color, almost a magnolia shade, it turns a fairly dark brown with age. The stem is 2–3 in. Several fans may grow from the same stem, rather like flowers. The gills are quite deep and run down the stem; they are white to light tan in color. The flesh is white and has a rather mealy smell. The spore print is lilac.

HABITAT AND SEASON

It grows in dense clusters on cut stumps of most deciduous trees, in particular elm, oak and beech. The season is spring to late autumn.

STORAGE

This mushroom air-dries well.

PREPARATION AND COOKING HINTS

If picked carefully, only a light wipe of the cap should be necessary. Discard most of the stalk as it will be quite tough, particularly where it was attached to the tree. The pleasant flavor makes it a good addition to all mushroom dishes.

gills run down the stem

often deep funnel-like cap

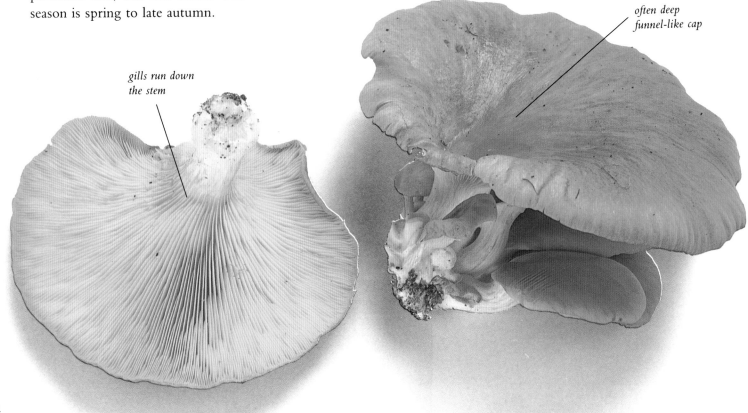

Pleurotus ostreatus

OYSTER MUSHROOM

BELOW *This is the gray-brown late-autumn/winter form of* Pleurotus ostreatus. *In summer, the cream-colored form,* P. pulmonarius, *is more common.*

Now grown commercially on a fairly large scale and so quite familiar, it is still exciting to find a wild oyster mushroom. They grow on dead or decaying trees, often in large masses. They will grow in the same place in successive years, so remember where you picked them.

IDENTIFICATION

The cap is 2½–4¾ in across. It is shaped rather like a fan and larger specimens may have fluted edges. The color can vary: usually a slate gray, they can sometimes have a slightly brown or bluish tinge. They have almost no stem. The gills run down the stem; pure white at first, they turn cream with age. The flesh is white with a pleasant smell. The spore print is lilac. Oyster mushrooms grow in groups, one on top of the other, and if carefully removed from the tree are usually very clean.

HABITAT AND SEASON

These occur in large clusters on standing trees or on the stumps of fallen trees. Most commonly found on beech trees, they will grow on other trees, especially elm. The season is all year round.

STORAGE

All methods of storage can be used for oyster mushrooms. If you separate the caps you can air-dry them very successfully.

PREPARATION AND COOKING HINTS

If picked carefully they are likely to be clean and a wipe with a damp cloth is probably all they need. The oyster mushroom's pleasant flavor means that it goes well with almost all meats and fish, making it extremely useful in the kitchen.

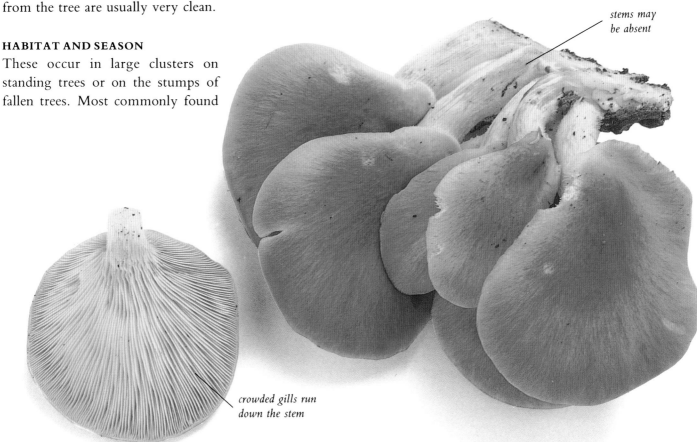

stems may be absent

crowded gills run down the stem

Russula cyanoxantha

CHARCOAL BURNER

The charcoal burner is an excellent mushroom to eat. However, it is a member of a very large genus and identification within the group can be very difficult. Correct identification is essential because some are poisonous, in particular the beechwood sickener, *Russula mairei*, and the sickener, *Russula emetica*. As always, if in doubt leave it out.

IDENTIFICATION

The cap is 2–7 in across and slightly greasy. Convex at first, it opens out with a shallow depression in the center. Occasionally a single color but more often than not quite a mixed shade, ranging from purple to light green, frequently with a rather faded appearance. The stem is 2–4 in and white. The gills do not run down the stem and are whitish or pale cream in older specimens. A clear identification feature of the charcoal burner is that the gills do not break away if they are touched, they are quite clearly joined to the cap margin. This is in marked contrast to some *Russula* species. The flesh is white and the smell is pleasant. The spore print is white.

HABITAT AND SEASON

Usually to be found under broad-leaved trees, but can also grow in association with pine trees. The season for the charcoal burner is summer to late autumn and it can be very common.

STORAGE

Drying is a very good method of storing the charcoal burner.

PREPARATION AND COOKING HINTS

It is rare to find a perfect specimen, as woodland wildlife attack it from almost the moment it appears. As a result it will need careful cleaning. However, it is good to eat whether fresh or dried and will add an interesting taste and texture to your mushroom dishes, as it retains quite a crunchy texture when cooked. But do remember to be careful with your identification of the charcoal burner and make sure it is not one of the poisonous *Russula* species.

cap is often of mixed colors or even green

stem is white, sometimes flushed lavender

crowded white gills

RIGHT AND BELOW *The dull violet-purple cap shown here is typical, but beware, the cap can also be completely green. The best means of identification is to brush your fingers over the gills and they should be flexible and not crumbly as most other Russulas are.*

BELOW *A large and colorful group of mushrooms, all Russula species. The mushrooms in this family are some of the most difficult to identify accurately.*

CAULIFLOWER FUNGUS

The cauliflower fungus is quite un-like any other fungus you will find in the woods. When you find one you will understand why it got its name. It is quite unusual, but grows in the same place year after year, so make a note of where you find it. One large specimen can last for several days if stored carefully in a cool place with its base in water.

IDENTIFICATION

The cauliflower fungus has no cap in the ordinary sense of the word, instead the fruit body is built up of many layers that resemble a cauliflower or a brain. A short stem attaches it to the tree on which it grows. The fruit body ranges from 7¾–19¾ in in dia-meter. It ages from a pale yellow-white to brown. It has a sweet smell and a lovely nutty flavor.

HABITAT AND SEASON

It grows on the roots of pine trees, very close to the trunks. Be careful not to cut too deeply when picking this fungus so as not to destroy the main mycelial growth from the roots; then you will be able to come back for more in subsequent seasons. *Sparassis crispa* is a western species; the eastern species is called either *S. spathulata* or *S. herbstii* and lacks a stem. It grows on old oak stumps as well as pine.

The cauliflower fungus grows from late summer to late autumn but is susceptible to frosts and so will be killed by the first frosts of winter.

STORAGE

This dries extremely well. Air-drying is probably best: hang your specimens up on strings in a light, airy place for several days. Very large specimens can be cut into sections so they will dry more quickly. As the fungi dry the insects and other life in them will fall out, so do not attempt to dry them in your kitchen; an airy

color varies from buff to creamy white

LEFT *Note the flattened crispy lobes. If they are pointed and branched you have probably mistakenly picked one of the* Ramaria *species which are often toxic.*

shed or outside storeroom would be best. Any hint of dampness will, of course, spoil the drying. It is very important to dry this mushroom thoroughly – be patient, it will be worth it.

RIGHT *The fruit bodies are almost always at the base of a tree or stump, as seen here.*

PREPARATION AND
COOKING HINTS

Pick only creamy white specimens, as this is when the fungus will be at its very best. Cleaning needs care as there are so many nooks and crannies in the cauliflower fungus and, as it grows so close to the ground pine needles can be a problem. If possible, avoid cleaning in water. It is better to brush away any dust particles, cut into thin slices and clean each slice before cooking. If you do use water, remember to dry the fungus well on paper towels before cooking. One of the nicest ways to deal with this fungus is to cut it in thin slices, dip them in a batter made with beer rather than milk and deep-fry to make a wonderfully crisp nutty hors d'oeuvres or accompaniment to a favorite dish. But it is equally good if sliced fresh and added to stews and casseroles.

edges of lobes turn brown with age

Suillus luteus
SLIPPERY JACK OR PINE BOLETE

The slippery jack is quite common and a good find, although its open texture makes it prone to insect infestation. Much prized by chefs, it is very versatile in the kitchen.

IDENTIFICATION
The cap is 2–6 in across; a nice mid-brown color with a marked sheen. It tends to be very sticky when wet, so is best picked in dry conditions. The stem is 2–4 in, pale yellow with a large, clearly visible ring. The pores are pale yellow. The flesh is white. It has no particularly distinctive smell. The spore print of the slippery jack is light brown. Only pick mature fresh specimens.

HABITAT AND SEASON
Found in association with conifers, particularly Scots pine. The season is late summer to late autumn.

STORAGE
Because of its soft texture, this mushroom is best thinly sliced and dried for use in winter dishes.

slimy surface when moist

pores unchanged by bruising

thick purple ring

PREPARATION AND COOKING HINTS

As the cap is slightly sticky in texture it is best peeled before use. Check carefully for insect infestation. This mushroom exudes quite a lot of juice when cooking, so it is a good idea to sauté it out first on its own. Strain well and keep the resulting liquid to be used later for a sauce. Then add the mushrooms to other dishes. Slippery jack can be used in many ways. One nice one is to mix the strained mushrooms with rashers of broiled or fried bacon, add the strained juice, thicken with a little flour and serve it on toast.

BELOW *This and other* Suillus *species are only found growing under conifers.*

BOTTOM *Observe how the cap colors change from young to old. The purple-brown turns pale to orange-brown with age.*

Suillus variegatus

Another useful bolete to add to your collection, although it is not as good to eat as the cep or the bay bolete. Only pick young specimens. They are quite light in texture and therefore can become insect-infested, so check specimens before collecting.

IDENTIFICATION
The cap is 2–4¾ in across and a rusty color. It is sticky when picked wet. The stem is 2–3½ in. The pores are quite clearly a snuff-brown color. The flesh is very white. The spore print is light brown.

HABITAT AND SEASON
Found almost exclusively with conifers. The season is from late summer to late autumn.

STORAGE
Best dried.

PREPARATION AND COOKING HINTS
A wipe of the cap is usually all that is necessary, but beware when slicing specimens to look out for insect infestation. A good addition to mixed mushroom dishes.

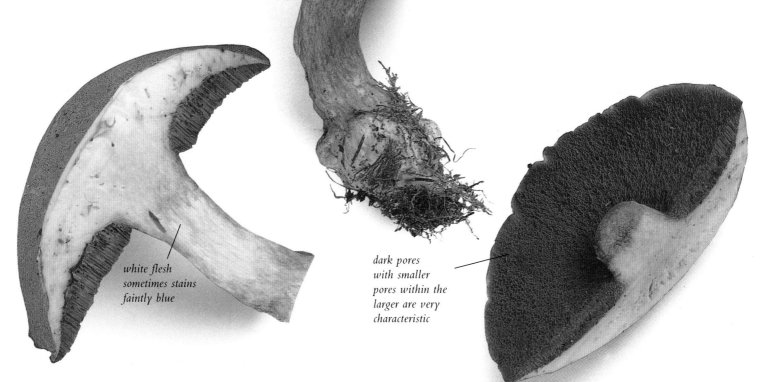

dry, slightly felted, scaly surface

white flesh sometimes stains faintly blue

dark pores with smaller pores within the larger are very characteristic

Tricholoma ponderosa
WHITE MATSUTAKE

BELOW *This large species has a single layered ring at the stem apex, some lookalike larger species will have double rings at the top.*

This is one of the larger mushrooms and is much favored by the Japanese. It is excellent whether eaten fresh or dried.

IDENTIFICATION
The cap is 1½–9¾ in across, convex becoming flat, with a broken margin. It is slightly inrolled at first, but opens fully with age. It has a smooth surface which feels quite tacky when dry. It is pale white and can be streaked with light brown. The stem can be up to 6 in; it is solid and is sheathed with a veil that runs from the cap to the base. It breaks in patches and can become pinkish-brown, and quite fibrous around the root. The gills are white, attached and crowded. The white flesh, which can stain light brown, has a slightly spicy smell. The spore print is white.

HABITAT AND SEASON
It is scattered in coastal areas in sandy soil and is usually found in conjunction with conifers. Not known to grow in Europe, it is common in western North America. The season is late summer to mid-autumn.

STORAGE
Drying is the best method of storage. Whole mushrooms can be dried quite easily, using an electric dryer, by hanging them up or by placing them on drying racks. Dried ones can often be found in Japanese and Chinese supermarkets.

PREPARATION AND COOKING HINTS
Likely to be clean when you find it, it will need little more than washing. It adds an interesting flavor to wild mushroom dishes, but is quite strident, so be careful what you use it with and how much you put in a dish. As it has a large cap, it is also ideal to be used for stuffed mushroom dishes.

Tuber aestivum

SUMMER TRUFFLE

Although summer truffles grow far more extensively than most people realize, finding them is difficult for they grow beneath the surface of the soil. Animals love them, particularly squirrels and deer, so watching them might give you a clue as to where to start looking.

IDENTIFICATION

The fruit body is ¾–4 in across. It is irregular, though roughly globe-shaped, and covered in a host of tiny black warts. It is blackish-brown in color. When cut through, it reveals a wonderfully marbled, reddish-brown interior. The smell is very distinctive and sweet and the taste is nutty.

HABITAT AND SEASON

The summer truffle favors calcareous soils and can be found in the ground near beech trees, and also, though less often, in association with sweet chestnuts and evergreen oaks. The season is late summer to autumn.

STORAGE

One of the best ways of storing truffles is preserving them in olive oil. First of all clean the truffle and shave off the skin which can be used in future recipes. Blanch the truffles very quickly before placing in oil in a completely air-tight container.

PREPARATION AND COOKING HINTS

As truffles have a very strong flavor they are best used in small amounts and even a tiny quantity can transform a dish. They are delicious served with egg and pasta dishes.

spores are dispersed by burrowing animals and insects

Tuber magnatum
THE PIEDMONT OR WHITE TRUFFLE

This must be the prize for all mushroom hunters. The most sought-after of the truffles, it is found in very limited areas, mostly in northern Italy, where the finest certainly grow. Unfortunately, highly trained dogs or pigs are necessary to locate it.

IDENTIFICATION
The fruit body is generally 2–4¾ in across, although much larger, tennis-ball-sized specimens do occasionally occur. It is irregular in shape and yellowish-brown in color. Indeed, in color and size it is not unlike a new potato. The flesh is marbled and has a slightly reddish-brown tinge. The smell is highly distinctive and sweet.

HABITAT AND SEASON
Just below the soil surface in mossy mixed woodlands. Its season is from late autumn through the winter to early spring. Due to its intense smell, it is found usually by dogs or pigs.

STORAGE
These truffles are best stored in closed containers and used fairly quickly after collecting. They have an intense flavor which can permeate foods, so use them to flavor eggs before cooking. Alternatively, put in a closed container with freshly made pasta and leave in the fridge overnight. This gives the pasta a most wonderful truffle scent. The best method of storage would definitely be in extra virgin olive oil. It will not only preserve the truffle but will flavor the oil and give it a wonderfully rich truffle taste. These are the most valued of the wild fungi and command extremely high prices. Excellent quality ones can be obtained from specialty importers, and the truffle oil, the fresh truffles or the truffles in extra virgin oil are well worth buying.

PREPARATION AND COOKING HINTS
Very little needs doing to the truffle beyond a careful brushing. If they are to be used fresh, very finely sliced slivers, quickly cooked, are best for the intensity of the flavor.

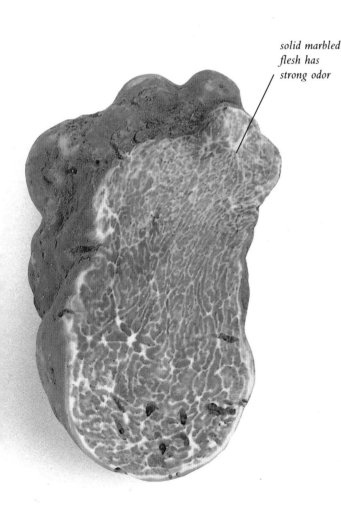

solid marbled flesh has strong odor

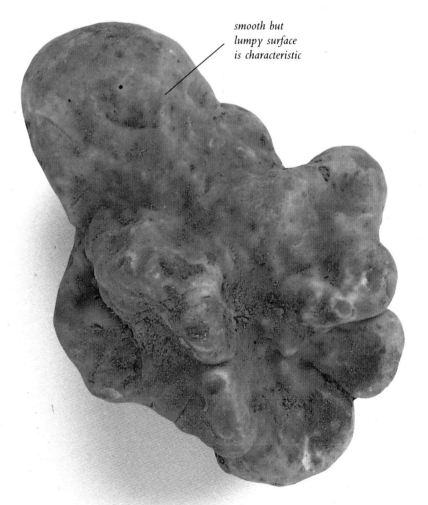

smooth but lumpy surface is characteristic

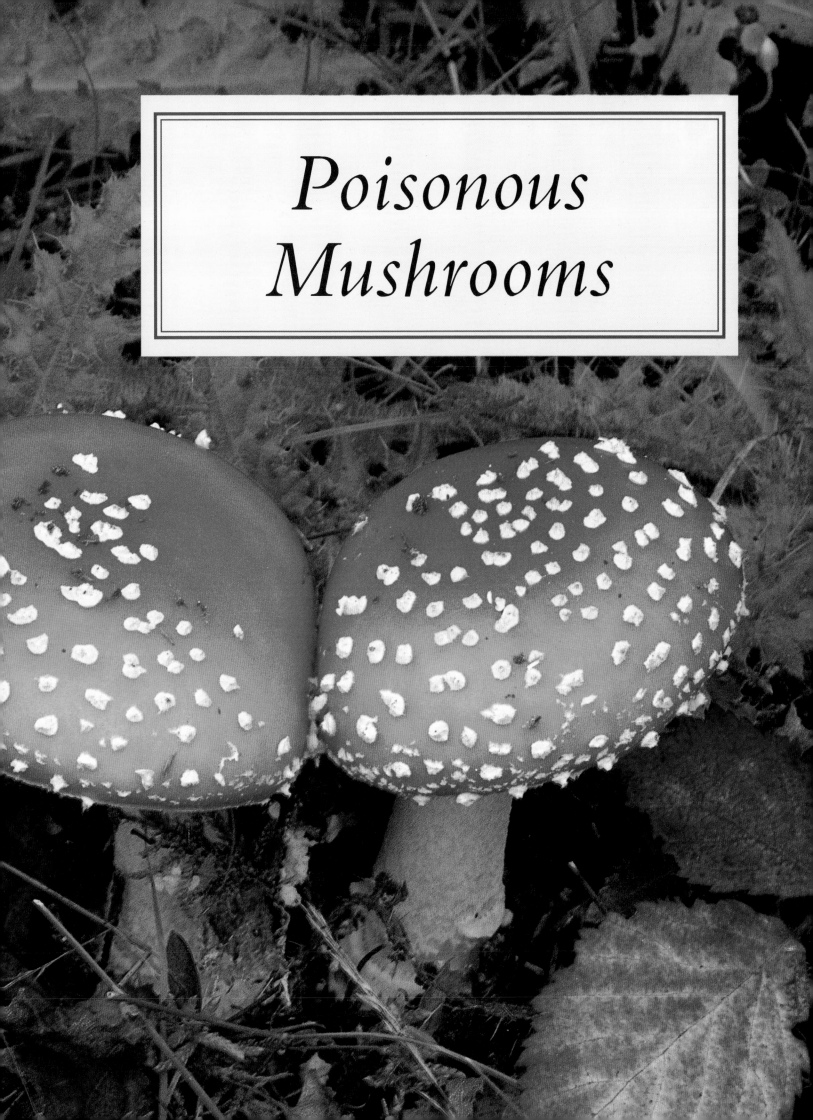

Poisonous Mushrooms

INTRODUCTION

Every year, in spite of repeated warnings, people die of mushroom poisoning. Such deaths emphasize the importance of identifying your mushrooms correctly. People often make the literally fatal mistake of assuming that if animals can eat a mushroom so can humans. Unfortunately this is untrue, for example, slugs eat death caps and other members of the genus *Amanita*. So do not be taken in when you see signs of either bird or animal activity; it is probably safe for them but may not be for you. Be particularly careful if dealing with the *Amanitas*, remember that their spores are poisonous and that if eaten they will cause extensive damage to the liver and central nervous system. If you think you are dealing with an *Amanita*, dig out the whole specimen with a stick to examine the volval cup. It is a good idea to protect your hand with a glove.

Never, ever, put a poisonous mushroom or an unidentified one with others in your basket. If you require a specimen for identification, put it in a separate container, and always wash your hands after touching any unidentified mushrooms. If you pick a deadly *Amanita* for display, throw out the mushroom and container immediately after use. A good way to transport and display such mushrooms is to put them in a plastic container on crumpled paper and to cover the whole box with plastic wrap. People can then see the mushroom without having to touch it. There are many old wives' tales about how to identify edible and poisonous mushrooms. They are all false. Particularly dangerous is the saying that if you can peel it you can eat it. You can peel a death cap, which got its name for a very good reason! Other sayings refer to staining silver spoons black. Ignore them all, and take great care over identification so that you can be sure of living to enjoy your mushroom trophies.

Between the good edible mushrooms and the deadly poisonous ones, there is an enormous range of other mushrooms regarded as inedible or not worthwhile. These are not all included in this book. Should you require information about them, consult one of the guides listed at the end of this book.

Although most people can eat the edible mushrooms and fungi identified in this book, it is important to remember that eating large quantities of any very rich food can often cause upset stomachs, and some people do have an adverse reaction to fungi. Among those that could cause problems are the wood blewit, *Lepista nuda*, and the field blewit, *Lepista saeva*. Should you ever become ill after eating mushrooms, it is important to see your doctor immediately. Mushroom poisoning can occur almost instantaneously or up to fourteen hours after eating the mushrooms, and at any time in between. It is imperative that you seek medical advice and, if possible, take a sample of the mushroom you have eaten. Correct identification of the poison could be life-saving, and there are many cases of *Amanita* poisoning being dealt with early enough to save the victim's life.

Another mushroom to beware of is the yellow stainer, *Agaricus xanthodermus*. A member of the genus *Agaricus*, it grows in similar situations to the ordinary field or horse mushroom and can be quite common in good mushroom years. Safety is the key for all collectors, so if you are not sure about a mushroom, leave it out of your basket.

LEFT Clitocybe rivulosa, *similar to the fairy mushroom but highly toxic.*

PREVIOUS PAGE *A typical group of fly agarics,* Amanita muscaria, *showing how the red pigment fades at the edges with age or after rain.*

OPPOSITE *The death cap,* Amanita phalloides. *The slight radial streaking on the cap can be seen well here.*

Agaricus xanthodermus

YELLOW STAINER OR YELLOW-STAINING MUSHROOM

The yellow stainer accounts for approximately 50 per cent of the cases of mushroom poisoning among those who pick either field or horse mushrooms. It has an unpleasant smell and taste and must be avoided at all costs. Identification can be difficult and therefore take careful note of the identification features and illustrations. The symptoms of poisoning are sweating and flushing with unpleasant stomach cramps. Not everyone is affected by the yellow stainer, but it is not worth taking any risks – leave it well alone.

IDENTIFICATION

The cap is 2–6 in across. Convex and angular at first, it flattens out later with a dip in the center. Very white

intense yellow stains on surface when scratched

cap becomes grayish and slightly scaly with age

mature gills turn brown

LEFT *Gardens, hedges and the edges of woodland are favorite habitats of this species.*

thick ring joins cap to stem

when young, it darkens with age as it expands to a fairly large cap with grayish-brown scales. It bruises a very bright yellow as soon as it is touched or cut, making this a valuable identification feature. Although this mushroom has many similarities with other members of the agaric family, the bright yellow staining is the giveaway. The stem is 2–6 in and white, staining bright yellow at the base. The gills are flesh-colored, darkening with age. The flesh is white. Smell is an important means of identifying this mushroom as it smells something like carbolic. The spore print is purple-brown. Should you have picked a yellow stainer by mistake and put it in your pan it will quite often turn the rest of the contents a slimy sickly yellow. It will also give off an acrid smell in the kitchen that is very unpleasant.

HABITAT AND SEASON
The yellow stainer grows in woods, pastures and gardens. It has quite a long growing season, from summer to late autumn. It is common in certain areas.

Amanita citrina and *Amanita citrina* var. *alba*

FALSE DEATH CAP

There are two forms of the false death cap, *Amanita citrina* and *Amanita citrina* var. *alba*. Although neither are deadly poisonous, they are so easily confused with the death cap that it is best to leave them alone.

IDENTIFICATION

There are two distinct forms of this fungi: one with a pale greenish-yellow tinge to the cap (*A. citrina*) and the other with a pure white cap. (*A. alba*). In both forms the cap is 1½–4 in across. It is usually covered with patches of the veil, which is one of the features that distinguishes it from the death cap which rarely has any veil remnants. The stem is 2½–3 in. It has a large basal bulb or cup where the remnants of the veil can be seen and it has a clear ring around the stem. The gills are off-white at first, darkening with age. The flesh is white. The spore print is white.

HABITAT AND SEASON

Grows in deciduous or coniferous woods, especially beech woods, but can be found in a large variety of locations. The season is from summer to late autumn and it is quite common.

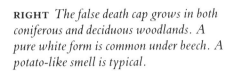

RIGHT *The false death cap grows in both coniferous and deciduous woodlands. A pure white form is common under beech. A potato-like smell is typical.*

veil fragments
mostly washed

bulb with
gutter-like
margin

BELOW *In this example, the prominent flat white patches of veil have washed off the cap leaving it quite smooth.*

Amanita muscaria
FLY AGARIC

Without doubt this is everybody's idea of a toadstool or poisonous mushroom. The little flecks on the red cap which sometimes grows to 7¾ in across make it quite distinctive. Many fables of myth and magic are associated with this mushroom. One, which sounds like a myth but is not, is its use by the Sami people of Lapland to round up their reindeer herds. They take advantage of the reindeers' liking for the fly agaric and scatter dried ones for the reindeer to eat, which makes them more manageable. The toxins contained in *Amanita muscaria* attack the central nervous system producing intoxication, hallucination and a euphoria that is similar to drunkenness. The poison stays in the system for several months but the symptoms generally disappear in twelve hours, although it may take several days to fully recover.

The only mushroom you are likely to mistake for *A. muscaria* is *A. caesarea*. However, *A. caesarea* has a large volval cup whereas *A. muscaria* does not. In addition, when cut lengthways, *A. muscaria* is white whereas *A. caesarea* is yellow. Another pointer is that the cap of *A. caesarea* does not show flecks of the remnants of the volval cup. When the volval cup finally breaks, it leaves *A. caesarea* clean. *A. caesarea* grows in limited locations throughout Europe except the United Kingdom.

IDENTIFICATION

The cap of the fly agaric is 3–7¾ in across, cup-shaped at first, it then flattens out. Although usually bright scarlet and covered with flecks of veil remnant, the color may fade in wet weather, and a few come up a fairly

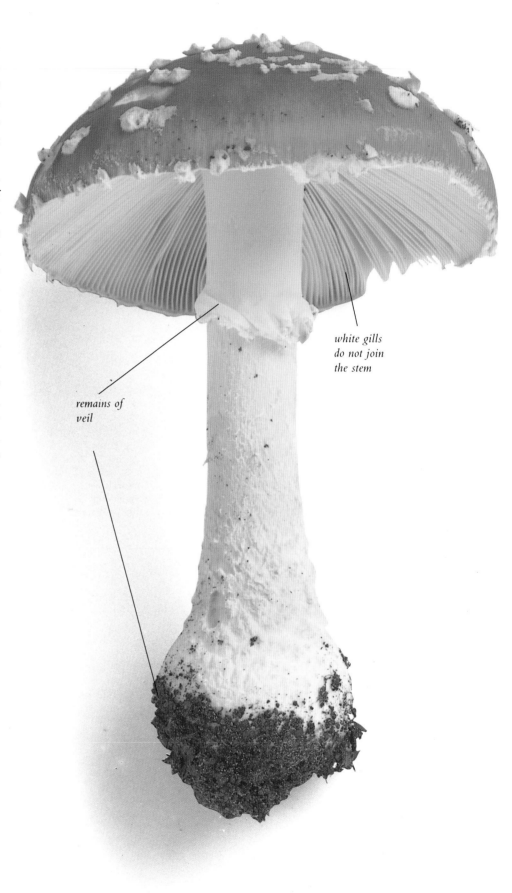

white gills do not join the stem

remains of veil

pale orange. The white stem is 3–7 in. If you take a specimen right out of the ground you will see the rounded, swollen stem base. (The gills are white.) The smell is indistinct. These often occur in fairly large groups at all stages of development. The spore print is white.

HABITAT AND SEASON

The fly agaric is most often found with birch trees, although it can occur with a wide range of trees and in many locations. The season is late summer to late autumn and it is very common.

BELOW *This is* A. caesarea, *which unlike the fly agaric has a clean cap and a sac-like volva.*

BOTTOM *After heavy rain, the flecks wash off the cap of the fly agaric and the red color fades to orange.*

Amanita pantherina

PANTHER CAP

Less common than the fly agaric, the panther cap, *Amanita pantherina*, too, is severely toxic. The greatest danger with the panther cap is that it can be confused with the blusher, *Amanita rubescens*. Many people eat the blusher after first cooking it to remove the toxins and then using it normally. However, it requires a very expert eye to distinguish between young specimens of the blusher and the panther cap, so it is best to avoid both species for fear of making a mistake.

IDENTIFICATION

The cap is 2–4 in across, almost bronze in color, and covered with small pure white remnants of veil. The margin also has remnants of the veil. The stem is 3½–5 in, white with a ring. It has a very bulbous base and narrow ring, very low down which

narrow, hoop-like ring low down on stem

pure white fragments of universal veil

one or more rings of tissue around bulb-like base

forms a distinct free rim around the base. There are usually also one or two belted rings immediately above the bulb. The spore print is white.

HABITAT AND SEASON
The panther cap grows with both coniferous and deciduous trees most-ly in western North America. The season is summer to late autumn, winter in California.

ABOVE *Beech woods on limestone soils are the favorite habitat of the panther cap although it will grow under coniferous trees as well.*

RIGHT *This picture illustrates the narrow hoop-like ring around the middle of the stem.*

DEATH CAP

Each year the death cap accounts for most of the fatal poisonings caused by eating mushrooms. It looks fairly innocuous, smells pleasant and can be peeled. However, it is deadly and only one cap is needed to cause serious, possibly fatal, poisoning. The range of colors can be quite dramatic, making identification even more difficult. It can vary from a sickly green to dark brown to pale white, so great care must be taken over identification. If you go on a foray, make sure the leader finds one to point out to you. If it is dug out of the ground you will see the volval cup at the base very clearly. Take a good look and remember what you see, for a large specimen can kill several people.

IDENTIFICATION

The cap is 1¼–6 in across. It is quite round at first, flattening with age. It has a smooth, almost shiny surface. The color is often greenish turning to a rather dirty brown, but beware, in wet weather the cap can become quite pale. The stem is 2–5 in and white. The gills are free and quite crowded; white at first, mature specimens may have an almost flesh-colored tinge. The flesh is white with a yellow tinge by the cap, and it smells quite sweet. The volval sac or cup is quite pronounced. The spore print is white.

HABITAT AND SEASON

Widespread in mixed deciduous woodland, particularly in association with oak. The season is early summer to late autumn.

The death cap deserves its name, it is the most deadly fungus known to mankind and years of research have not produced any antidote to the

white unchanging gills

olive cap may sometimes be white or yellowish

white, cup-like volva surrounds stem base

RIGHT *The caps often have a slightly radially streaked or fibrous appearance.*

poison. Many have tried and some people have been saved by having their blood screened through charcoal, once the hospital had identified it as *Amanita* poisoning. The symptoms of poisoning take between 10 and 24 hours to become apparent, but during that time the poison has been attacking the liver and the kidneys. The first signs of poisoning are prolonged sickness and diarrhoea with severe abdominal pains; this is often followed by a period of apparent recovery when all seems well. However, death from liver and kidney failure will occur within a few days. There is a rare form of *A. phalloides* which is *A. phalloides* var. *alba*. Apart from being pure white throughout, which makes it look deceptively like an innocent mushroom, the features by which you will identify it are exactly the same and it is just as deadly.

ABOVE *The volva at the stem base may be completely hidden under the leaf litter, as seen here – beware!*

LEFT *Always carefully clear away around the stem base to expose the remains of a volva.*

Amanita virosa
DESTROYING ANGEL

Like many *Amanitas*, the destroying angel grows from a volval cup. It is deadly poisonous and well deserves its name, being white and fatal. The symptoms of the poison are the same as for *Amanita phalloides*.

IDENTIFICATION
The cap is 2–6 in across, bell-shaped at first, it becomes very irregular when open. It is pure white. The stem is 3½–4¾ in and grows from a fairly large volval cup that is not regular at the base, but can clearly be seen with the fungus growing from it. There is a white ring which is very fragile and often incomplete. The gills are pure white. The flesh is white and the smell is slightly sickly. The spore print is white.

HABITAT AND SEASON
Grows in mixed deciduous wood-land and is happily not as common as the death cap. The season is usually midsummer to autumn. If you are on a foray, this is another mushroom that you should ask the leader to point out to you, for once seen you will be unlikely to forget it.

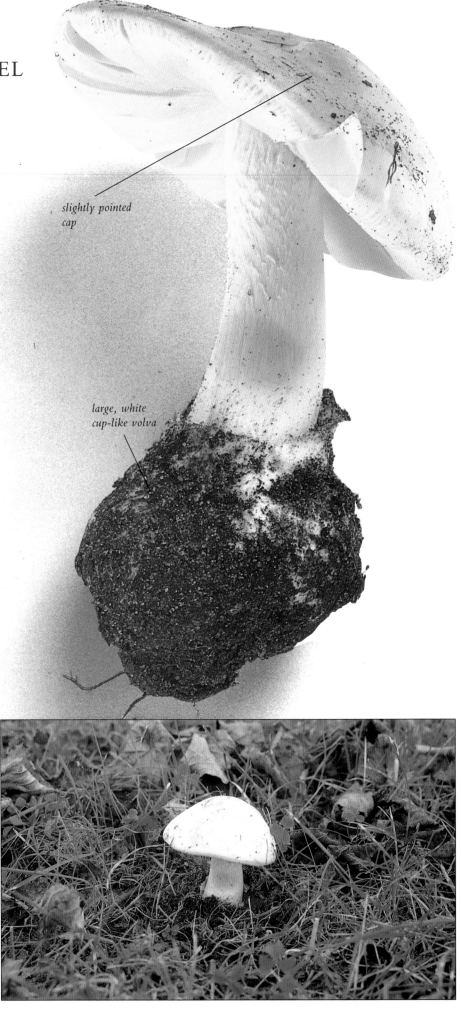

slightly pointed cap

large, white cup-like volva

RIGHT *The cap of this species often has a distinct hump or blunt point at the center.*

Clitocybe dealbata

BELOW *This shows the rather frosted appearance of the white caps and the slightly decurrent gills.*

Do not be fooled by this innocent-looking little mushroom, it is severely toxic. It often grows in just the places that many edible mushrooms grow (*n.b. Marasmius oreades*).

IDENTIFICATION

The cap is ¾–2 in across, flat with a depression slightly inrolled and fluted round the edge. It is off-white in color. The stem is ¾–1¼ in and whitish. The gills are quite crowded and run part way down the stem. They are almost cream in color. The flesh is white and it has a mealy smell. The spore print is white.

HABITAT AND SEASON

Grows in lawns, pastures and old meadows, often in groups or rings. It can be also be found in open woodland. The season is summer to late autumn and it is quite common.

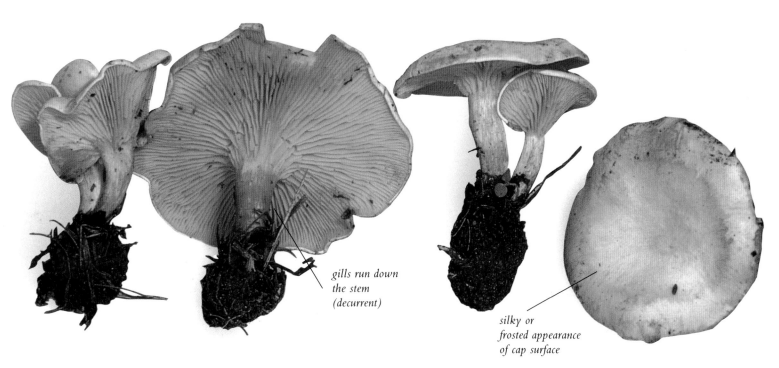

gills run down
the stem
(decurrent)

silky or
frosted appearance
of cap surface

Clitocybe rivulosa

BELOW Clitocybe rivulosa *mushrooms are usually a silky grayish-white, as here.*

Another innocent-looking, but severely toxic mushroom that can easily be confused with the edible fairy ring mushroom, *Marasmius oreades*. Both grow in rings, in similar sites and at much the same time of the year. Indeed it is not uncommon for rings of each species to grow within a few yards of each other. So take care. It would probably be a good idea to seek out live examples of both before you start picking the fairy ring mushroom.

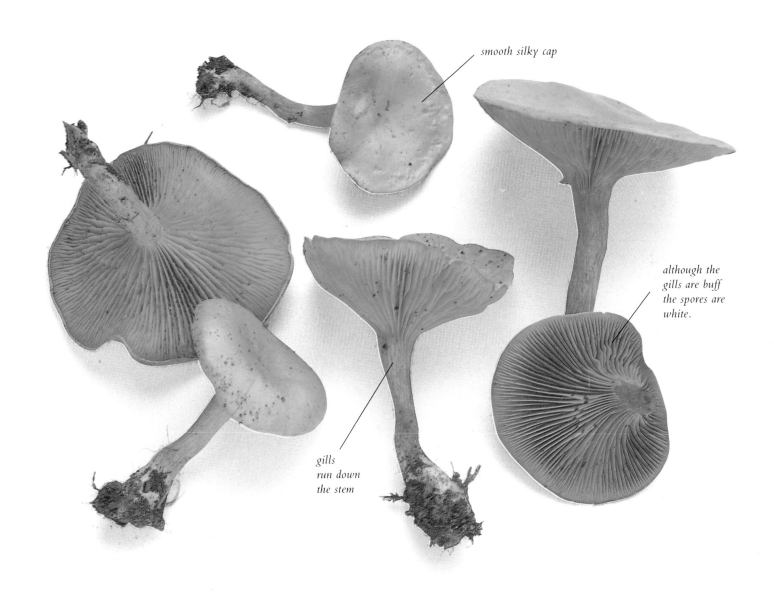

smooth silky cap

although the gills are buff the spores are white.

gills run down the stem

slightly funnel-shaped cap

gills are crowded

HABITAT AND SEASON

In groups or rings in sandy soil amongst grass, beside paths and roads. The season is late summer to late autumn and it is very common.

BELOW *These caps are rather waterlogged and so appear browner than normal. Usually they are a silky grayish-white.*

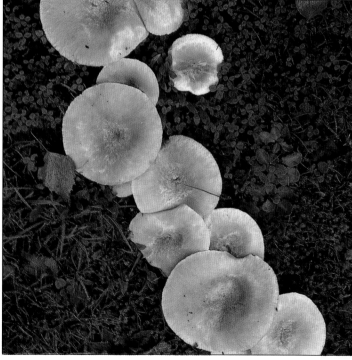

IDENTIFICATION

The cap is ¾–2 in across; cup-shaped at first, it soon flattens out with a small depression in the center. The margin remains slightly rolled. It is gray and concentric rings are visible. The stem is ¾–1½ in and a similar color to the cap. The crowded, gray gills run part way down the stem. The flesh is dirty white to gray. The closeness of the gills and the color and shape of the cap are important ways to distinguish this mushroom from the fairy ring mushroom. The spore print is white.

Coprinus atramentarius
COMMON INK CAP

The common ink cap or alcohol ink cap is not poisonous in itself, but if eaten in conjunction with alcohol, it can cause alarming symptoms, such as nausea, palpitations and stomach cramps. For this reason it has been used over the years in attempts to cure alcoholics. The ink cap gets its name from the fact that it was used many years ago by monks to produce an exceptionally fine drawing ink, made by boiling the collapsed inky caps with a little water and a hint of cloves. The difference between the common ink cap and the shaggy ink cap is quite marked, but it is important that you recognize this one for it would be a catastrophe to make a mistake at a party at which you were serving alcohol. Young specimens of the magpie fungus, *Coprinus picaceus*, could be confused with the common ink cap. Although not as common as this, it grows in fairly large quantities in the late summer to autumn. It is best avoided because although not poisonous, it can cause nausea and vomiting in some people.

gills blacken and liquify when mature from the edge inwards

note brown scaly base to stem

IDENTIFICATION
The cap is ¾–1½ in across, white and bell-shaped. Light gray to grayish-brown in color, with veil remnants often attached to the cap. The stem is 2¾–6¾ in and white. The gills are crowded, white at first, they change from brown to a dark inky mass. The smell is not distinctive. The spore print is brown.

HABITAT AND SEASON
The common ink cap grows in tufts, often in association with buried wood. The season is from spring to late autumn and they are very common, often growing in large groups.

LEFT *This is one of the most common species in towns, gardens and woodlands everywhere, often associated with dead or buried wood.*

Galerina autumnalis
DEADLY GALERINA

This fungus is deadly poisonous and must be avoided. The poisoning is very similar to that of the *Amanita* family.

IDENTIFICATION
The cap is 1–2¾ in across. It is convex at first, becoming flat with a slight dome at the center. It is a dark brown fading to a light buff with age, and when moist is quite sticky and shiny. The hollow stem is ¾–4 in and fairly bulbous at the base. There are slight brownish to blackish markings at the base of the stem, and the mycelial threads are clearly visible at the bottom. There is a veil that breaks fairly easily and is quite small. The gills are attached and quite close, yellowish in color, becoming redder with age. The flesh is off-white. The deadly galerina has no smell. The spore print of the deadly galerina is dull orange-brown.

HABITAT AND SEASON
The deadly galerina tends to live on well-decayed coniferous or deciduous wood, often in quite large groups. Its season is from late spring to autumn through winter, depending on the zone. The deadly galerina is not known in Europe, but common in North America. The very similar *G. marginata*, however, is common in Britain and is equally deadly.

ABOVE *Note the brownish-yellow gills which distinguish this from edible species such as the honey mushroom. The gills of the honey mushroom often darken in age, but they always have white spores.*

Hygrophoropsis aurantiaca
FALSE CHANTERELLE

Although not poisonous in the way that agaric and amanita mushrooms are, the false chanterelle is known to cause gastrointestinal problems.

IDENTIFICATION
The cap is ¾–3 in across, flat at first with a slightly inrolled margin, it becomes more funnel-shaped with age. In large specimens the cap is more fluted and looks much more like a chanterelle. However, the false chanterelle's cap is orange rather than the yellow of the true chanterelle. The gills are dark orange, close and run down the stem. The spore print is white.

ABOVE AND RIGHT *The false chanterelle is very common under both pine and birch trees, and the cap becomes funnel-shaped with age.*

crowded
gills are
soft and often
forked

cap margin
inrolled when
young

HABITAT AND SEASON
Grows in coniferous woodland and on scrubland. It is very common and often grows in groups close to chanterelles. The season is from summer to late autumn.

Hypholoma fasciculare
SULPHUR TUFT

This is a very common mushroom and grows all the year round, even in the winter. It is not deadly poisonous, but definitely should be avoided. It could be confused with other fungi, such as honey mushrooms, *Armillaria mellea*, and brick cap, *Hypholoma sublateritium*, that are extremely good to eat, so take care with your identification.

IDENTIFICATION
The cap is ¾–3½ in across and is convex. The remains of the yellow veil often adhere to the margin. The cap itself is bright yellow with a dark orange center. The stem is 1½–4 in, curved and a similar color to the cap. The gills are first bright yellow, but turn dark sulphur-green, then brown with age. The flesh is bright yellow, becoming brownish near the base of the stem. It has quite a mushroomy smell. The spore print is purple-black.

HABITAT AND SEASON
This occurs in dense clusters on the rotting timber and stumps of deciduous and coniferous trees. It grows throughout the year.

note purple-brown spores deposited on stem

BELOW *One of the most common fungi everywhere on dead or dying wood, the sulphur tuft grows in large clumps.*

Inocybe patouillardii
RED-STAINING INOCYBE

The red-staining inocybe is severely toxic and therefore must not be eaten. Many of the others in this family are poisonous, if not as deadly as this one, therefore it is best to avoid all the inocybes.

IDENTIFICATION
The cap is 1¼–4 in across, slightly conical and uneven. The margins are often cracked, giving the typical appearance of an inocybe. Cream-colored, the cap has red-staining fibres. The stem is 1¼–4 in, fairly thick and slightly bulbous at the base. The gills are quite pink at first, like those of a mushroom, and then darken to a light brown color. The flesh is white and has no particular smell. The spore print is dull brown.

HABITAT AND SEASON
Grows along paths in mixed woodland on chalky soils, especially those with beech and, less often, chestnut. The season is spring to late autumn.

RIGHT *The white fibrous cap and stem, with blood-red stains when bruised, are very distinctive. The red-staining inocybe likes open woodlands on alkaline soils.*

Lactarius pubescens

Lactarius pubescens is a member of the large milk cap family. It is important to be able to identify this mushroom for not only is it a strong emetic but it can be confused with the edible saffron milk-cap *Lactarius deliciosus*. The woolly edges of *Lactarius pubescens* are an important feature of identification.

IDENTIFICATION
The cap is 1½–4 in across, convex and slightly depressed with the margin markedly inrolled and woolly at the edge. It is often quite pale to rose pink; but this tends to fade in direct sunlight. The stem is 1¼–2½ in and a palish pink. The gills are crowded, light pink and tend to darken with age. They run down the stem. The flesh is quite thick and whitish, but can have a pinkish tinge. There is no particular smell. Equally common and shaggy is *L. torminosus*, a brigh-

ter pink and equally upsetting if eaten. The spore print is creamy-white.

HABITAT AND SEASON
This mushroom tends to grow fairly widely but often near birch trees on fairly poor or sandy soil. The season is from late summer through to late autumn.

gills bleed white milk when cut

funnel-shaped cap

Paxillus involutus

POISON PAXILLUS

ABOVE *A mature cap with margin unrolled.*

The poison paxillus is a very common mushroom. It is also severely toxic. It can have a bolete-like shape, which makes matters worse, some bolete species being, of course, edible. The toxins have yet to be identified, but their effect is somewhat similar to leukemia.

IDENTIFICATION

The cap size is 2–6 in across. It is quite flat when young, becoming convex and somewhat funnel-shaped with age. It gets its name from its clearly inrolled rim. This color is mid- to red-brown. The cap is slippery when moist and shiny when dry. The stem is up to 3 in and similar in color to the cap. The narrow, crowded gills are yellow turning brown to red-brown when bruised. The gills run down the stem. The spore print is sienna.

HABITAT AND SEASON

The poison paxillus grows beside paths in broad-leaved woodland, especially with birch, and on quite acid scrubland. It has a long growing season from summer to late autumn.

ABOVE *This is an immature cap with tightly rolled cap margin.*

crowded
gills
bruise brown

inrolled
margin

Russula emetica
THE SICKENER

There are at least 150 different species of *Russula*, making it one of the largest groups of fungi. Some, such as the charcoal burner, are edible, but many are highly poisonous. The sickener and the very similar looking beechwood sickener, *Russula mairei*, did not get their names without good reason. It is really best to leave this family well alone.

IDENTIFICATION

The cap is 1¼–4 in across and is cup-shaped, later flattening with a shallow central depression. The cap is a brightish red, but sometimes has faded white areas. When peeled, it shows red-colored flesh underneath. The white stem is 1½–3½ in. The gills are creamy, darkening slightly with age. The flesh is thin and fragile and can be quite sticky. It is white except under the cap. The smell is sweet and fruity. The spore print is whitish.

BELOW *The sickener is found under pines, especially in wet areas.*

HABITAT AND SEASON

Grows almost exclusively under pines. The season is summer to late autumn and it is very common. As its name suggests, the beechwood sickener, which has a similar season, grows almost exclusively under beech trees.

pure red
cap skin peels
off very easily

flesh is
brittle and crumbly

widely spaced gills

GLOSSARY

asci The sacs in Ascomycetes in which the sexual spores are formed.

Acomycetes Group of fungi characterized by bearing the sexual spores in a sac (asci).

Basidiomycetes Group of fungi characterized by the presence of spore-bearing cells called basidia.

brackets Shelf-like fruit bodies.

cap The portion of the mushroom bearing the gills and the tubes.

convex A surface that is curved or rounded outwards.

decurrent Running down the stem.

fibrous Composed of fine fibers or threads.

flesh Inner tubes of a fungus.

fruit body Structure on which the spore-producing cells are held.

hymenium Layer of spore-producing cells.

inrolled Curled inwards and down.

marginate With a distinct ridge or gutter-like margin.

milk Sticky fluid released by some fungi when damaged.

network A mesh or pattern of criss-crossed fine ridges.

partial veil The fine web of tissue connecting the cap margin to the stem.

pores The openings of the clustered tubes in Boletes and Polypores.

recurved Curving backwards, i.e. scales with recurved tips.

ring Remains of the partial veil left on the stem.

scales Small to large raised flakes or flaps of tissue, usually on the cap or stem surface.

spore Reproductive cell of typical mushroom.

spore print A thick deposit of spores dropped by a mushroom cap onto paper.

stem The 'stalk' on which a mushroom cap is raised up.

striated With distinct parallel grooves or lines especially at the cap edge.

tubes The downward pointing clusters of tubes on Boletes and Polypores within which the spores are produced.

universal veil The fine to thick covering of tissue which envelopes some fungi when immature.

volva Example of thick universal veil which remains as a sac at the base of the stem.

OPPOSITE *Horn of plenty*, Craterellus cornucopioides.

LEFT *Saffron milk-caps*, Lactarius deliciosus.

INDEX TO FIELD GUIDE

Numbers in bold indicate the main entry.

A

Agaricus arvensis (horse mushroom), 11, **26**, **27**

Agaricus augustus (the prince), **28**

Agaricus bisporus, **29**

Agaricus campestris (field mushroom), 16, **30**, **31**

Agaricus macrosporus, **32**

Agaricus silvaticus, **33**

Agaricus silvicola (wood mushroom), **34**

Agaricus xanthodermus (yellow stainer or yellow-staining mushroom), 27, 32, 34, 99, **100**, **101**

Aleuria aurantia (orange peel fungus), **35**

Amanita caesarea (Caesar's mushroom), 104, 105

Amanita citrina (false death cap), **102**, **103**

Amanita muscaria (fly agaric), **104**, **105**

Amanita pantherina (panther cap), **106**, **107**

Amanita phalloides (death cap), 98, **108**, **109**

Amanita rubescens (blusher), 106

Amanita virosa (destroying angel), **110**

Amanitas, 34, 98, 99

Amethyst deceiver (*Laccaria amethystea*), 25, **62**

Anise mushroom (*Clitocybe odora*), **50**, **51**

Armillaria mellea (honey mushroom), 25, **36**, **37**

Ascomycetes, 10, 11

Auricularia auricula (Tree ear or wood ear), 16, **38**, **39**

B

Basidiomycetes, 10, 11

Bay bolete (*Boletus badius*), 14, 25, **40**

Beefsteak fungus (*Fistulina hepatica*), 11, 23, 25, **56**, **57**

Black morel (*Morchella elata*), 25, **80**, **81**

Black trumpet (*Craterellus cornucopioides*), 54, 55

Blue leg (*Lepista saeva*), 16, 25, **74**, **75**, 99

Blusher (*Amanita rubescens*), 106

Boletus badius (bay bolete), 25, **40**

Boletus chrysenteron (red-cracked boléte), **41**

Boletus edulis (cep or porcini), 11, 17, 19, 25, **42**, **43**

Brick cap (*Hypholoma sublateritium*), **61**

Brown birch bolete (*Leccinum scabrum*), **70**

C

Caesar's mushroom (*Amanita caesarea*), 104, 105

Calocybe gambosa (St George's mushroom), 16, **44**, **45**

Cantharellus cibarius (chanterelle), 14, 19, 25, **46**, **47**

Cantharellus infundibuliformis (winter chanterelle), **48**, **49**

Cauliflower fungus (*Sparassis crispa*), 11, 59, **88**, **89**

Cep (*Boletus edulis*), 11, 17, 19, 25, **42**, **43**

Chanterelle (*Cantharellus cibarius*), 14, 25, **46**, **47**

Charcoal burner (*Russula cyanoxantha*), **86**, **87**

Chicken of the woods (*Laetiporus sulphureus*), 11, 16, 25, **66**, **67**

Clitocybe dealbata, 78, **111**

Clitocybe fragrans, 51

Clitocybe odora (anise mushroom), **50**, **51**

Clitocybe rivulosa, 17, **112**, **113**

Collecting mushrooms
    cleaning, 18

    equipment, 18, 19
    method of, 19
    places for, 14
    time for, 16, 17

Common ink cap (*Coprinus atramentarius*), **114**

Common morel (*Morchella vulgaris*), 81

Coprinus atramentarius (common ink cap), **114**

Coprinus comatus (shaggy ink cap), **52**, **53**

Coprinus picaceus (magpie fungus), 53, 114

Cortinarius, 73

Craterellus cornucopioides (horn of plenty or black trumpets), **54**, **55**

Craterellus infundibuliformis (winter chanterelle), **48**, **49**

D

Deadly galerina (*Galerina autumnalis*), **115**

Death cap (*Amanita phalloides*), 98, **108**, **109**

Deceiver (*Laccaria laccata*), **63**
Destroying angel (*Amanita virosa*), **110**
Drying mushrooms, 20

F

Fairy ring mushroom (*Marasmius oreades*), 16, **78**, **79**, 112
False chanterelle (*Hygrophoropsis aurantiaca*), 46, **116**

False death cap (*Amanita citrina*), **102**, **103**
Field blewit or blue leg (*Lepista saeva*), 16, 25, **74**, **75**, 99
Field mushroom (*Agaricus campestris*), 16, **30**, **31**
Fistulina hepatica (beefsteak fungus), 11, 23, 25, **56**, **57**
Flammulina velutipes (velvet shank) 16, **58**
Fly agaric (*Amanita muscaria*), **104**, **105**
Forays, 25
Freezing mushrooms, 20, 21

G

Galerina autumnalis (deadly galerina), **115**
Galerina marginata, 115
Giant polypore (*Meripilus giganteus*), 67

Giant puffball (*Langermannia gigantea*), **68**, **69**
Grifola frondosa (hen of the woods), **59**

H

Hedgehog fungus (*Hydnum repandum*), **60**
Hen of the woods (*Grifola frondosa*), **59**
Honey mushroom (*Armillaria mellea*), 25, **36**, **37**
Horn of plenty or black trumpets (*Craterellus cornucopioides*), **54**, **55**
Horse mushroom (*Agaricus arvensis*), 11, **26**, **27**
Hydnum repandum (hedgehog mushroom), **60**
Hygrophoropsis aurantiaca (false chanterelle), 46, **116**
Hypholoma fasciculare (sulphur tuft), 61, **117**
Hypholoma sublateritium (brick cap), **61**

I

Identification of mushrooms, 25
Inocybe patouillardii (red-staining inocybe), **118**
Ink cap (*Coprinus atramentarius*), **114**

L

Laccaria amethystea (amethyst deceiver), 24, **62**
Laccaria laccata (deceiver), **63**
Lactarius deliciosus (saffron milk-cap), **64**, **65**, 119
Lactarius pubescens, 64, 65, **119**
Lactarius torminosus (woolly milk-cap), 64, 119
Laetiporus sulphureus (sulphur polypore or chicken of the woods), 16, 25, **66**, **67**
Langermannia gigantea (giant puff-ball), **68**, **69**
Leccinum aurantiacum, 14
Leccinum scabrum (brown birch bolete), **70**
Leccinum versipelle (orange birch bolete), 14, **71**
Lepista nuda (wood blewit), 16, 25, **72**, **73**, 99
Lepista saeva (field blewit or blue leg), 16, 25, **74**, **75**, 99
Lycoperdon excipuliforme, 69

M

Macrolepiota procera (parasol mushroom), 53, **76**
Macrolepiota rhacodes (shaggy parasol), **77**
Magpie fungus (*Coprinus picaceus*), 52, 53, **114**
Marasmius oreades (fairy ring mushroom), 16, **78**, **79**, 112
Meripilus giganteus (giant polypore), 67
Morchella elata (black morel), 25, **80**, **81**
Morchella esculenta (morel), 25, 80, **82**, **83**
Morchella vulgaris (common morel), 81
Morels (*Morchella esculenta*), 25, 80, **82**, **83**
Mushroom poisoning, 99

O

Orange birch bolete (*Leccinum versipelle*), **71**

Orange peel fungus (*Aleuria aurantia*), **35**
Oyster mushroom (*Pleurotus ostreatus*), 16, **85**

P

Panther cap (*Amanita pantherina*), **106**, **107**

Parasol mushroom (*Macrolepiota procera*), 53, **76**

Paxillus involutus (poison paxillus), **120**

Pickling mushrooms, 21

Piedmont truffle (*Tuber magnatum*), **95**

Pine bolete (*Suillus luteus*), **90**, **91**

Pleurotus cornucopiae, 84

Pleurotus ostreatus (oyster mushroom), 16, **85**

Pleurotus pulmonarius, 85

Poison paxillus (*Paxillus involutus*), **120**

Polyporus frondosus (hen of the woods), **59**

Prince, the (*Agaricus augustus*), **28**

R

Red-cracked bolete (*Boletus chrysenteron*), **41**

Red-staining inocybe (*Inocybe patouillardii*), **118**

Russula cyanoxantha (charcoal burner), **86**, **87**

Russula emetica (the sickener), **121**

Russula mairei, 121

S

Saffron milk-cap (*Lactarius deliciosus*), **64**, **65**, 119

Salt preserving, 21

Shaggy ink cap (*Coprinus comatus*), **52**, **53**

Shaggy parasol (*Macrolepiota rhacodes*), **77**

Sickener, the (*Russula emetica*), **121**

Slippery Jack (*Suillus luteus*), **90**, **91**

Sparassis crispa (cauliflower fungus), 11, 59, **88**, **89**

Sparassis herbstii, 88

Sparassis spathulata, 88

Spore prints, 13

St George's mushroom (*Calocybe gambosa*), 16, **44**, **45**

Storing mushrooms, 20, **21**

Stropharia aeruginosa (verdigris agaric), 50, 51

Suillus, 14

Suillus luteus (slippery jack or pine bolete), **90**, **91**

Suillus variegatus, **92**

Sulphur polypore (*Laetiporus sulphureus*), 11, 16, 25, **66**, **67**

Sulphur tuft (*Hypholoma fasciculare*), 61, **117**

Summer truffle (*Tuber aestivum*), **94**

T

Tree ear (*Auricularia auricula*), **38**, **39**

Tricholoma nudum (wood blewit), **72**, **73**

Tricholoma ponderosa (white matsutake), **93**

Tuber aestivum (summer truffle), 10, **94**

Tuber magnatum (Piedmont or white truffle), **95**

V

Velvet shank (*Flammulina velutipes*) 16, **58**

Verdigris agaric (*Stropharia aeruginosa*), 50, 51

W

White matsutake (*Tricholoma ponderosa*), **93**

White truffle (*Tuber magnatum*), **95**

Winter chanterelle (*Cantharellus infundibuliformis*), **48**, **49**, 55

Wood blewit (*Lepista nuda*), 16, 25, **72**, **73**, 99

Wood ear (*Auricularia auricula*), **38**, **39**

Wood mushroom (*Agaricus silvicola*), **34**

Woolly milk-cap (*Lactarius torminosus*), 64

Y

Yellow stainer or yellow-staining mushroom (*Agaricus xanthodermus*), 27, 32, 34, 98, **100**, **101**

ADDRESSES OF MYCOLOGICAL SOCIETIES

North American Mycological Association
Kenneth Cochran, Executive
Secretary, NAMA
3556 Oakwood
Ann Arbor, MI 48104–5213
313–971–2552
E-mail: Internet:
KWCEE@UMICH.edu

**COMA
Connecticut Mycological Association**
c/o Sheine
930 Old Mill River Road
Pound Ridge, NY 10576–1833

Illinois Mycological Association
13535 Longview Drive
Lockport, IL 60441–9440

Boston Mycological Club
Karen Davis, Corresponding
Secretary
470 Washington St.
Holliston MA 01746

Cercle des Mycologues de Montreal
4101 rue Sherbrooke
Montreal PQ Canada – 2B2

BELOW *Horn of plenty,* Craterellus cornucopioides.

Puget Sound Mycological Society
University of Washington
Urban Horticulture #GF–15
Seattle, WA 98195–0001

Mycological Society of San Francisco
P.O. Box 882163
San Francisco, CA 94188–2163

Texas Mycological Society
7445 Dillon Street
Houston, Texas 77061–2721

BIBLIOGRAPHY

ARORA, DAVID, *Mushrooms Demystified* 2nd ed., 10 Speed Press 1986.

BESSETTE, ALAN AND WALTER J. SUNDBERG, *Mushrooms: A Quick Reference Guide to Mushrooms of North America*, Field Guide Series, Collier Books, Macmillan 1987.

DICKENSON, COLIN and LUCAS, JOHN, ed., *The Encyclopedia of Mushrooms* Putnam 1979.

LINCOFF, GARY H., *The Audubon Society Field Guide of North American Mushrooms*, Chanticleer Press, Dutton 1978.

LINCOFF, GARY H., and GIOVANNI PARIONI, ed., *Simon and Schuster's Guide to Mushrooms*, Simon and Schuster 1981.

MILLER, ORSON K. JR., *Mushrooms of North America*, Chanticleer Press, Dutton 1978.

PHILLIPS, ROGER, *Mushrooms and North America: The Most Complete Guide Ever*, Little Brown 1991.

SMITH, ALEXANDER and NANCY S. WEBER, *Mushroom Hunter's Field Guide*, University of Michigan Press 1980

nb. There are now some excellent regional mushroom guides. If you don't have a university or a mycological society nearby, go to your local library or bookstore and check the *Subject* volume to *Books in Print*. In 1994 there were listed many such guides to the different regions of North America. They are very useful additions to the general guides.

ACKNOWLEDGEMENTS

The publishers and authors would like to thank the following people for their help in the production of this book: Geoffrey Kibby of the International Institute of Entomology, London; Andrew Broderick of the Australian Wild Fungi Research Group, School of Horticulture, University of Western Sydney, Hawkesbury, Bourke Street, Richmond NSW 2753 Australia; Clive Houlder, mushroom hunter and supplier of specialist fungi; L'aquila Products, 40 Caledonian Road, London, for providing the truffles; Valerie Jordan and Avril Henley for their help in typing the manuscript; Mycologue, 35 King Henry's Road, London, for providing the knives; Patricia Michelson, La Fromagerie, 30 Highbury Park, London N5 2AA, specialist food finder; Taste of the Wild, 65 Overstrand Mansions, Prince of Wales Drive, London SW11 4EX, suppliers of wild mushrooms.

Picture credits

t = top, b = bottom, l = left, r = right
Heather Angel page 103br
Timothy J. Baroni 111t, 111b
George Dickson 45t, 45b, 118
Geoffrey Kibby 67tl, 70t, 83, 81tl
George McCarthy 2, 6/7, 15b, 17t, 22/23, 24, 28l, 28r, 29b, 34, 35b, 47b, 59t, 59b, 61t, 63m, 65b, 73t, 77b, 82tr, 82r, 96/97, 98, 106, 107l, 107r, 113b, 246
Gregory Mueller 31b, 61b, 63b, 66/67, 81b, 82l, 93, 115
Oxford Scientific Films (David Thompson) 29t; (G I Bernard) 30, 31t; (Jack Dermid) 105t

BELOW *Winter chanterelle,* Cantharellus infundibuliformis.

128